# FOREWORD

From my childhood I took great pleasure in words and rhythms. Loving
effectiveness of the spoken word, verse-speaking and reading aloud ga
cherish the memory of a particular reading-at-sight class in an eisteddfod when, at the age ot 1U, I
managed to pronounce 'misled' as 'measled' and 'concise' as 'konkize'. It wasn't funny at the
time - well, at least, not to me!)

I went on to read English at King's College London, followed by the acquisition of a P.C.G.E. and a
career spent teaching English, and directing a range of plays in what passed for my spare time. In
1960, before accepting an invitation to teach in Africa for three years, I put my house in better
order and acquired Licentiates in Speech and Drama from the Guildhall School of Music and
Drama and Trinity College London. Then what a revelation it was to discover and nourish the
natural performing arts of my Ugandan students! On retirement from teaching in 1990, I had the
time to extend my L.T.C.L. to a Fellowship.

The new leisure also gave me the opportunity to explore more music and I had always loved to
sing. Participation in many courses at home and abroad during the next thirty years has enriched
me beyond measure. It has been a privilege to work with a galaxy of brilliant and engaging
conductors, and exciting to share such experience with so many like-minded enthusiasts-turned-
friends. The repertoire has been largely, but by no means exclusively, Early Music, from Gregorian
chant - which I loved from the moment I heard it and have sung from my teens - to the early
eighteenth century. The Renaissance, in particular, has been a focal point. So many of these
Course Directors have been not only superlative musicians but witty and articulate wordsmiths
whose bons mots I would covertly scribble all over my score, lest I forgot. The resulting poems
which form most of the first section were usually delivered at the farewell meal after the final
concert.

The second section of hymns and carols is a selection from the verse I have written at various
times in an effort to tell 'the old, old story' again in words that have immediacy without banality,
dignity free of archaism or cliche. I hoped that they would prompt those who sing them to
visualise afresh. (I believe passionately, in any case, that it is crucial for any singer, soloist or
other-wise, to embrace the text in order to express it: the melody is fundamentally a vehicle for
the words.) To illuminate the over-familiar and make it newly vibrant was always the intention here.

Among these pieces are several translations from the Latin originals. 'Angelus ad Virginem' was
always a great favourite of mine, words wedded beautifully to the accompanying melody, and I
wanted to make plainchant recessionals like 'Puer natus est in Bethlehem' available to those with
no Latin. The little Aztec cradlesong, 'Xicoche Conetzintle', is exquisite musically and my English
version, written primarily for programme elucidation, exactly fits the rhythms of the existing
setting.

I have brazenly used the familiar words 'Forty Days and Forty Nights' by G.H. Smitten and F. Pott
as the starting point for my own Lenten hymn. The first 8 lines and the last 4 are substantially the
same as the original but in between I have depicted the three temptations in detail. The resulting
8-line stanzas double the original unit and I wrote a complementary tune for lines 5-8 which
'responded to' and developed from the 'Heinlein' melody of the original.

The final section is a ragbag of pieces, most of which were written for friends over the years or to express my enjoyment of place names or linguistic oddities.

There are also one or two poems relating to the current scene: the threat of terrorism is ever with us and Covid 19 may have been somewhat scotched but not yet killed. But, in spite of all, let us be cheered and fortified by the inexhaustible pleasures of words and music, and of shared laughter.

Finally, and most recently, a poem for the Queen's great Jubilee, an occasion of real national celebration.

Jill Mitchell, June 2022

III                      SUNDRIES AND OCCASIONALS

## GRATIAS!

My most grateful thanks are due, first of all, to John Greenhalgh, my primum mobile, who persistently nudged reluctant and technophobic me into action and has subsequently collated and organised all the material I provided. I am also greatly indebted to my friends Elaine Kilmurray, Cath Cainen, Ged Glover, Tony Horner, Christine McCann, Chrissie Papavasilopoulou, Sallie Rankin, Kate Scally and Mary Whitehead who have painstakingly retyped these poems.

# APOLOGIA

'THUS NATION SHALL SPEAK UNTO NATION', THEY CRIED,

'AS RADIO RANGES THE WORLD, FAR AND WIDE'...


COMPUTERS, ALAS, DO NOT ALWAYS CONVERSE

WITH EQUAL FACILITY, CAN BE PERVERSE,

AND SOFTWARE TO SOFTWARE CAN DROP THE ODD STITCH,

PRODUCING DISCREPANCY, ERROR, AND GLITCH.

SO HOW MAY I PILOT THIS SMALL CRAFT TO ANCHOR

WITHOUT AN AVAILABLE LINGUA FRANCA?

TO ALL NAVIGATION IT'S STUBBORNLY DEAF:

'YOU CANNOT RE-EDIT IT FROM PDF!'

THESE VERSES WERE PROCESSED FROM MULTIPLE SOURCES

FROM GENEROUS FRIENDS, GIVING TIME AND RESOURCES.

FOR EVERY ANOMALY, ODD VARIATION

OF FORMAT, OF SPACING, OF SIZE, OF CITATION,

SUCH QUAINT INCONSISTENCY PRAY YOU EXCUSE;

YOUR KIND MAGNANIMITY DO NOT REFUSE!

# CONDUCTORS (AND SINGERS) IN ACTION

## Nos 1-24

WHEN DAVID HEARD . . . .

"D Major's good to start the daily drill,
It's choc-a-bloc with healthy Vitamin C;
For hangovers,  F Major is just brill!
Depend on that, and take it straight from me . . .
Let's drop the notes into the little sack
That nestles at the bottom of the back,
And fill with air right down to base of spine;
With this balloon of ballast, you'll be fine.
Some vowels are good to tone and flex the lips,
But Elvis-rolling loosens up the hips.
Now limbered-up, the job is halfway done,
Alert, prepared, we're ready now to run . . .
The Tallis needs a frame of mind that's ZEN          -
It is a vast steam-roller of a piece -
But William Byrd is something else again,
Quicksilver, madrigalian caprice!
For Byrd you must be primed and circumspect,
Agility of mind and speed of eye,
Or only realise in retrospect
You missed the moment as it scudded by.
-But that was Byrd from Poundstretcher, not Heal's
Or Harrod's.  Give full measure.  No cheap deals!
Be stylish!  Put yourselves into your parts,
Give 'character',  with intellect and hearts.

Perk up, you chaps;  you're moving at the speed
Of motorways upon Bank Holidays.
Take off the handbrake!  Purposefully feed
Into the traffic-flow with no delays.
You're fumbling in your pockets for your change,
Commitment-time!  These notes are in your range!
- Aargh!  THAT was like a neck-less Cheshire cat!
Don't overshoot.  Take care on that E flat,
You Tenors – there, the tuning was . . exotic -
Moreover, the effect is quite quixotic
When you produce your own polyphony,
Unaided by the rest – calamity!
Approach that top A, Tenors – here's the wheeze! -
With buttocks clenched.  Give them a further squeeze,
You'll reach that note to which you here aspire -
And with some luck, the ruse will not backfire!

I haven't seen the whites of one chap's eyes
All day.  Oh, thank you.  That's a nice surprise.
But what a shame: as we pick up the score
Again he's gazing firmly at the floor.
I'm sorry, ladies, you have sat around
For ages while the gentlemen rehearse;
But it was vital to evolve a sound
Not like a sow's ear but a silken purse.
Princesses' mattresses have peas beneath,
Not hunks of rampant rhubarb from the heath.
- It still is somewhat rustic, yes indeed,
Evoking lorry-loads of chicken feed,
And yet just now we'll make no further move,
But put it under a wet towel to 'prove'.

Make sure the et was truly anacrusic
Or you will simply not be making music,
For all the sense and shape goes out of joint,
When filius that's datus is the point ! . .
While benedictus breathes an air celestial
The pleni's almost jaunty and terrestrial!
It must really swagger, like a catwalk dolly -
Not limp, like a crone with a tartan trolley.
The spiky lines should scamper, hover, sprint,
The consonants should fly and flash and glint.
- Ah, that was splendid.  That was really good -
Here have a refill of this lemon pud.

From A to top D in two bars is wide,
Sopranos hold tight for a bumpy ride!
Your quality's 'vanilla', over-bland;
I need a rather less sand-papered brand
Of sound on top, Sopranos – rich and oaky;
Don't do anaemic-pale, but boozy-smoky.
HERE, Seconds, on the 'Bakewell' you're the 'cherry':
This cadence, then, is extrovert and merry!
C naturals THERE are eyebrow-crinkling stuff,
Sopranos; milk them more.  It's not enough,
Now brush some olive oil across that phrase
And  leave it on the oven shelf to glaze . . "

We're mortified: we've dropped a minor third,
We're quite done in: our tuning was absurd.
"Those chords, you know, were just a load of bollocks
Like wild-splashed canvasses of Jackson Pollock's!"
And, like a mournful foghorn, Andrew blows
The unforgiving sackbut to expose
Relentlessly, so that we writhe and twitch
The hideous discrepancies of pitch.

"Look Basses, here's another of my tips:
Do try to match the ladies' languid lips,
And on that miserere make a little
Moo-moo shape, with dash of toffee-spittle . . .
Just fling those phrases, Altos, round your head
Like wildly drunken aunties at a wedding,
Not hanging back, as waiting to be led
All tentative, and cautious where you're treading.
Toss out the notes insouciantly!   Risk it!
That's better:  Have yourselves a chocolate biscuit.
Your bottom F, though, had a luscious tone,
Perhaps you've earned a bit of Toblerone."

So, warts and all,
We're on the ball,
With knees that spring,
And hearts that zing,
Our thoughts on 'NING',
We're set to sing
From head to toe replete with jeu d'esprit,
When we take off anon for Malmesbury!

Jill Mitchell<br>Lacock,

31.12.2006

# CANTANDUM (HILARITER!) CUM CARLO

Let's try today to keep off politics –
Us Spaniards and our wily, knavish tricks –
No talk of 1588,
A most humiliating date,
Armada issues we'll resist –
We are not bitter, we insist!

Now may we look more closely at this part;
That really was an unconvincing start.
Of that whole phrase, it is the first
Of all those notes which is the worst.
THINK of that note already floating there –
It should be somehow present in the air –
So take a breath and relish with the nose
(Imagine that you sniff a fragrant rose)
Your face expectant, ready, and alert,
Your mouth prepared, in shape, and not inert,
With buoyant, focused mind, and poised in limb,
The body, brain and spirit all in trim,
Then vocalise with skilful registration –
But, Basses, you are lost in your vibration,
And so you offer low-geared, unsupported
Sound.  Can you refine that, get it sorted? …
And now you're not together, it appears:
Use less projection, utilise your ears,
(Why are you so at odds and no one hears?)

You're NOT in canon here – now who began it?
Which was the satellite, and which the planet?
Who made an error? Let it be admitted!
Who doesn't even know what she committed?
Mistakes should be possessed of style and dash,
Effected with conviction and panache,
Not stumbled through with weak passivity,
But full of positive activity,
So make them, please, with energy and verve,
At least you're holding nothing in reserve …
I thought this was in four parts;  you contrive
In your perversity to make it five!

Sopranos, you are sounding most unsure;
Sing out with certainty!  No, give me MORE!
And don't look at me with such desperation.
Why IS there all this feeble hesitation?

Your faces drained, and strained with mute appeal –
How, you imagine, does that make me feel?
You must, to start with, get the rhythms right
Or else you'll crash-land from a dizzy height.
No words, then;  clap the patterns first of all
Or, jumping between buildings, you will fall.
I don't want any corpses on the way
And, if precipitate, you'll go astray.

What am I going to do about these men?
The Basses shifting furniture again:
In atmosphere of heavy, stolid gloom,
They're shuffling clumsy cupboards round the room ….
Sybille, your sackbut's a bit aloof:
Imagine there are pigeons on the ROOF!
Go for it!  Urgent, resolute attack,
Ensure those pesky creatures don't come back!

Now **HERE** there is an atmosphere of awe,
As humble pilgrims marvel and adore,
And **THERE** a note of desperate petition
For mercy, and for sinful acts' remission;
And **NOW** – 'O LUX' – a joyful celebration
Of SAN JACOBE's lustrous elevation.
But you suggest a wholly different scene
Of minds unkindled and of dull routine.
'IN ILLO TEMPORE THERE WAS …. a CACTUS? –
That seems to be your textus contrafactus!
Unless you THINK the sense and concentrate,
How can you possibly communicate?
And all these moods should be expressed in faces,
Eyes and voice – and that includes the Basses!
Imagine, and articulate, and bring
Some breath of pulsing life to what you sing;
Involve yourselves wholeheartedly;  engage
With what you do.  Command your stage
At point of entry;  prove what you're about.
Be confident;  abandon every doubt,
Your manner and your mood assured and warm;
Behave as if this were your daily norm,
Possess the space – and radiantly PERFORM!

# TRUST ME, I'M THE CONDUCTOR

## Jill Mitchell

### With 'Cardinall' Carwood
### in Andalucia

*Jimena de la Frontera, April 2005*

There are a few details I ought to mention
That would repay your serious attention...
The Altos have picked up some subtle sign
That leads them to prefer their speed to mine.
Now, leave me to conduct and call the tune –
You could regard that as some sort of boon.
You're lab'ring on in such a stolid slow-grind,
Apparently those minims make you snow-blind.
Trust me, trust me! I'm the one conducting
And *ad libendum*'s thoroughly disrupting...
Now what was *that* pedantic phrase about?
Too many heavy accents stretched it out.
Your reasoning, p'raps, was theological,
When *apostolicam* near ground to halt.
But I believe it quite illogical,
Nay – vestra culpa! – 'twas a grievous fault.
A whole bar, Ladies, to look up at me
(My shirt this morning is a joy to see)
Make contact early, gaze upon my face:
Your entry will fall perfectly in place.

Bass quality I need that's full and round,
A Vienna-Philharmonic-cello sound;
It's totally *emulsioned*, Basses: read the signs,
Point up the verbal accents, shape the lines.
Don't mindlessly give thump to the first beat,
The textual rhythm isn't quite so neat.
The accent often doesn't coincide,
And bar-lines prove themselves a doubtful guide.
You often have to be prepared to find
Important syllables have been consigned
To *wrong* parts of the bar, so note these latter
And seek the crucial ones that really matter...
Do not announce the Saviour's joyful Rising
In tones that savour more of curdled milk,
Evoking moods of boredom, or chastising
(And memories of Father Charlie Dilke).
Let vowels be bright, and pure Italo-Latin
And consonants be clean as polished rapier;
Your mouths, alas, seem stuffed with silky satin
(And bring to mind dear Father Michael Napier).

On *per prophetas*, Sops, I'll buy your *dim*,
But your consumptive frailty is grim:
You sound about to teeter and expire,
Dames aux Camélias we don't require!
Power it through – the phrase is on the move –
Dress it with purpose, rise above the groove;
For loud and quiet singing, I would claim,
Are both, in all but one respect, the same.
*Piano* does not signify more tame,
Or rhythmically listless, lank, and lame.
Beware those dotted crotchets, as I've said;
Don't let them lose momentum, bulge and spread.
Keep their integrity, their rhythmic spring
With drive and with direction as you sing.
Supply the consonants, but keep the flow:
*They*'re music too. Don't break the line, but grow.
And on those quavers please don't rush: be steady! –
As I have told you several times already.
Those *Mimi* tones again! Oh, Sops, you must
Endeavour to be healthily robust,
Not languorous, tubercular, effete –
Like wilting wantons, robbed of life and heat...

Forget to breathe, and life is rendered fraught –
It might become significantly short –
And, Gentlemen, grouped thus behind me here
Your poor ensemble can't escape my ear.
You'll get away with nothing there, I fear;
Each wobbly hesitation's loud and clear.
That second beat was lazy, uninvolved,
And going nowhere – tension quite dissolved!...
As one, with proper preparation, prime
Your breathing to be perfectly in time.
Your first note then will scarcely fail to please
Me with its well-produced and focused ease.
Remember, too, I have some great upbeats,
So be prepared for *dic nobis* repeats, –
No, Basses – trust me – yet again you're late;
But Tenors, you were quite immaculate!...
These pointers listened to, and not ignored,
Victoria and Vivanco will applaud
(In heavenly and harmonious accord)
Our celebration of their Easter Lord.

## CARWOOD IN FLAGRANTE

Ladies, Gentlemen, this is a first!
This double bill will surely quench your thirst
For ne'er before, I hazard, has been found
Nick Ludford close with Palestrina bound.
What contrasts these great masters juxtapose,
For Ludford dazzles, Palestrina glows:
Flying melismas, awesome and immense,
Then the Italian's ardent eloquence.
Thus I can promise you a lavish feast
So let's begin, we'll make a start at least,
And, as your melody lifts high, think low;
When low, think high, and counterbalance so.

Oh, Tenors, there you really did me proud,
You're fabulous – but yet a tad too loud.
Be merciful, soft-pedal-down those yells
Or Altos will be drowned in decibels.
Basses, you sing a different language now,
Your vowels are just a shade agrarian -
Not that I favour "Prithee, how brown cow?"
But can you sound a trifle less...barbarian?
If you can make your vowels more Latin-pure,
The Sops will tremble at your rare allure.

GAUDIUM ANNUNCIAVIT'S meant
To be ecstatic, not belligerent,
So make that entry less aggressive, please –
But not perfunctory like journalese:
This news is of unprecedented worth,
Not bound for Peckham, merely, but the Earth,
So sound elated and not slightly bored –
Still too much Tenor in that final chord!
Don't charge on like express chuffers
Till you crash into the buffers;
Remember, too, it never pays
To clout the last note of the phrase.
The pulse, however, must not waver
So attenzione! Watch it!
For you're fast on every quaver
And late on almost every crotchet.
Have I not, Altos, cherry-picked with you?
Don't worry. Later you will get your due.

Pre-emptive breathing makes me nervous lest

You plan to enter early on a rest.
Don't overbreathe or underbreathe; have care
To take enough but not excessive air.
But it is crucial that you breathe in time,
You have to throw the ball up ere you serve,
The process should be ordered like a chime,
The breath contributes to the rhythmic curve....
That was brilliant – till bar 30, Basses,
Then you patently ran out of luck;
The notes were right but living in wrong places
So the whole thing sadly came unstuck.
Your second dotted minim needs more lengthS
And rhythmical precision, note, is strength.

Altos, don't rewrite bar 53.
Sopranos, do review that second G
And make it match the first one; and don't clump
Like that on 29 with such a thump.
Why did you do that? That was something new.
I can't imagine what got into you.
The Ds are *natural*, too; the As are *flat*!
I'll start to flap if you don't master that...
Now, bravely, Altos: these are notes you know,
Not separate and spiky then; a *line,*
And on those quavers don't so strongly *bow,*
The brilliance of Baroque is soon to shine...
If I were ultra-critical, I'd say
Your second beat with mine is not au fait...
That's charming, Altos. Now you're in your prime,
Quite beautiful – and very near in time!

Can you sound happier, you Gentlemen,
That Vergine Chiara is at hand
To hear the prayer you make with passion, when
In such dire need? How can you be so bland?
For half our problems would be promptly solved
If you could sound a little more involved.
In chant, above all, don't *produce* each note
But find the shapes, and let the phrases float
In rise and fall without pedantic stress,
Or music will be lost in *busyness*.

How comes it, Basses that you failed to see
The ladies were incensed at 73?
Have you not seen Sopranos when they're riled?
You'd be advised to keep them sweet and mild.

Amazingly elastic, I must say,
Your concept of the pulse appears today:
The Tenors woeful-slow in 72,
In 85 again they're overdue,
The Altos on 'electa', too, are late,
Sopranos – loth to sing at 88.
Much earlier there was a bit to fix…
Yes, there was something wrong at 26.
In GRATIAS, we must as one proceed
From syllable to syllable to pass.
Be circumspect, I urge: the ladies need
To show discretion where they place their 'as'.

Now we must rise above these feeble ruts,
I long to praise you all without the 'buts',
I've lauded you as wonderful and bright,
COULD YOU NOT PUT A FEW OF THESE THINGS RIGHT?

Monteconero June 2006

# AN INTERRUPTED CADENCE?

Our grand conductor, man of verve and vision,
Required of us less volume, more precision,
He said he wanted energy, not power.
He hoped, he said, that when the concert hour
Arrived the 'O Ja!' moments would be past,
That chaos would be clarity at last.

"Now that was almost beautiful!" he'd say,
"Perhaps it will be on another day.
Give me a tone that's gentle but direct,
Remember C is not  a pushed-up B,
And all the Sops and Tenors must agree
On where it is, and tune it to effect...
Tenors, if you don't intend to sing
F sharp, then please eradicate all doubt;
Don't leave your puzzled audience wondering
Just what it is you think you are about.
Make your mistakes with confidence and style,
Then I shall find it much less of a trial;
Don't trail away, be tentative and waver,
And do beware that undernourished quaver!...
We have a problem where First Tenors tend
To wallow in legato while the 'Twos'
Are rhythmical and agile. Where's the blend?
Is not the object perfectly to fuse?
The choirs must function at the self-same speed,
And syncopation there I do not need.
Democracy in music's a disaster,
Don't try to force the pace and make me faster.
Is it to be your tempo, then, or mine?
Stop thinking! Trust the beat and you'll be fine.
I promise you I'll be the one to win,
Bear that in mind as you again begin.
Can you involve your molars when you sing
And make impression for a dental plate?
'Sit laus' should have both clarity and weight
And in your very cheek-bones it should ring.
Oh dear, it's sounding rather drear, deflated,
So spin the wheel, be positive, elated...
One note escaped attention, Tenors, then:
There was a C sharp in a certain bar,
You'd better run that passage through again
And sort out where the accidentals are.

In fact, I hear some accidentals crushed;
Make space for them, allow them larger air;
And, Second Sops, the tempo there is rushed,
Do not accelerate; there's room to spare...
Come on! Don't hatch those eggs; be trumpets, Basses,
Spin high your tone and keep alive the line;
You people there, don't show me your fish-faces!
Be ready, for your moment comes to shine.
You start that section well but then derail;
Keep constant contact with me or you'll fail...
I'm grateful that you've helped me learn this piece,
You've taught me much, and caused me to increase
My grasp of it, enlightened me somehow;
I think I know it rather better now."

But, as for us, we've had a breathless time
And twenty years have reached their final peak
In these great Vespers, brilliant, sublime,
An unforgettably inspiring week.
So JanJoost, Martin, Marco we acclaim:
A splendid 'tres in unum' you have made,
Collaborating with a focused aim,
What radiance and energy displayed
(And quietly at keyboard Stephen stood
And played with utmost skill, and saw it good.)
Our soloists have thrilled and moved us too:
How rapturously Monteverdi floats
And shimmers in such hands! Our debt's to you
For you have given us so much more than notes.
This is the last of all our Lacock summers,
To which from far and near have flocked all comers.
What hoards of treasured music we have aired,
What friendships have been made, what laughter shared.
But future there will be in some new guise;
Unthinkable that such delight and grace
Should end. The phoenix surely shall arise
And reinvent itself, so watch this space.

On this glad note, end crisply all your parts:
Begone before the *Ritornello* starts!

# JJ – and the 'making' of Hay

Not every tenor heard what I just said!
Please listen to this plea and then apply:
An '*f*' does not mean crude and vertical—
Not *loud* but *fuller* sound, with tone enriched,
For *forte*'s a dynamic not glued on;
It grows organically from within,
And *dim*, remember, does not mean a *rit*,
Where all the energy disintegrates;
What is required is focus on the vowel—
A close-up-and-increased intensity.
*Piano* simply does not mean: 'Slow down,
Be less committed!—Many times, by countless
Fraught conductors, have you heard it said.

Please make a clear attack, so that your note
Does not require repair when halfway through.
Be vigorous, but don't let it unravel;
Stay strong in saddle, feel the heartbeat firm,
And heartbeat equals heartbeat—do not give
This piece a heart-*attack*; keep drumbeat stable!...
Basses, you *may* start on your own note!
Tenors, you're slightly changing key at (3)
('And notes from her great engine thundered out').
'I cannot grow. I have no shadow' must *sing*
Yet not slow down. *Sustain*, Sopranos, and be smooth,
Not clipped, staccato. (8) again!
And when we come to 'Weep, O weep away
The stain', remember, Burgi: *Tits to God*!
On final, dying notes ('immortal fire')
Stop with the diaphragm and not the throat—
It's more effective and more musical!

I noticed, Tenors, there was puzzlement—
(Bar (45) in the *cilicio*)—
Regarding how to pitch that quaver-group.
Just look at it—we'll run it through again...
I do not want to hear Sopranos *think*
As they negotiate with conscious care
Those twinkling ornaments at (31).
Don't think, Sopranos; see, and shape, the whole!

Oh, Altos, give direction to those quavers—
They should bear promise, moving to a shape…
There must not be a faceless wall of sound;
More clarity of rhythmic detail is
Required. Do not lose interest in those long
Extended notes, but 'upper case' the vowel.
The note must spin with higher revs and lots
Of air to gather energy and purpose.

Look, 'flats' are *not* 'low notes'; they have a different
Life and force-field; but on you they have
A drastic psychological effect
With negative result, depressing pitch,
And very soon a semitone is lost
Although I 'flute' a constant reference note
In urgent bid to pull you back on track...
*Regina Coeli* must not lose its pulse;
The quavers tick away like Switzer clocks
And with exact precision fill the space.
Don't let them lag behind, or lose their shape
And meaning. Keep momentum & control.

We've lost another semitone, but still
There is a little atmosphere at last—
For that, at least, I offer gratitude…
You're fighting with my tempo yet again—
As if you're weighing something else in mind!—
And do stop the conducting, Jill: I feel
I'm being challenged. Please, I ask you, don't!...
Make sure you keep in touch at cadences!
Conductors have their moments: *These* they are,
And we decree how they should be approached.

Enjoy your coffee! Contemplate your sins—
For many-fold they are, as well you know;
And afterwards, attempt to get things straight—
Or you will think 'O Ja! Oh dear!'—too late!

Hay-on-Wye
January 1st, 2011

## UN TRANCIO DI ROBERTO
### *(A Helping of Hollingworth)*

We've got a bit less than a week
In which to make this music speak
And reach some sort of modest peak.

No 'English' consonants then please:
Discard those wet, obtrusive Ts,
Those clumsy, thickly-plosive sounds
In which our native tongue abounds.
Just let the lines more fluid grow
And, as you sing, resolve to show
(throughout this 'sacred conversation'
From choir to choir in syncopation –
Despite the presence of antiphony)
The smoothness crucial to polyphony.
       The pulses are organic,
       So try to be less manic –
       No need for any panic.
Stretch out those vowel sounds with care
Then, at the bar line, spring for air.
But be not loth, tenacious Second Bass,
       To let the hapless dotted minim go;
Relinquish it with rather better grace
       And don't obstruct the forward lyric flow.
Seize not the notes in such a vice-like grip –
As if they meant to give you all the slip!
       And let us have 'an Ely m'
       When we are singing words like *Spem-m*
       *In alium-m*
       *(Or lilium convalium?)*

*Vigilias* requires more vim:        *Guami In die tribulationis*
This man's sleep has eluded him,
All rest denied and spirits dim …
<u>Here</u>, grief is desolate and deep,
So *plangite* must yearn and weep …     *Croce O triste spectaculum*
First Sops, a little 'mousy', that:
Be bright and resonant, not flat.
Just focus forward t'wards the nose,
Or Andrew must once more transpose!
Don't force me yet again to stop,
You'll know I'll register each flop.
Remember always as we go:
Soft palate high and larynx low.
If you persist in breathing late,

You'll find the music will not wait,
And if you take a quaver rest,
The train will not stop on request.
But, at the risk of sounding petty,
Your lumpy phrasing's like spaghetti;
There mustn't be excessive stress,
Your accenting must be much less.
What's more, your Ss are a mess.
To spread and splodge them isn't nice:
They must be neatly clean, precise.
So keep me constantly in view
That you may pick up every cue,
And, as I wave my arms above you,
Project to me: 'Dar-r-ling, I love-a-you!'

Venice, March 2004

# MEDITATIONS OF A MAESTRO:
### Robert Hollingworth's 'Advanced' course at OBIDOS.  Easter 2006.

C OMMISSA MEA cleaves the air –
It sounds like the conductor's prayer:

"In that I fail, I blush for shame
But sue for mercy just the same.
I cannot fathom what has chanced,
Performance should be much enhanced,
I piped to them: they have not danced
Yet, Lord, they deemed themselves 'advanced'.
My purposes they have deformed
And all my lofty aims are stormed;
The Garden of my Earth's Delight
Subsumed to pain and endless night.
Iniquity that nought can wash
Reaps its reward: remember Bosch
(Even Venus and Adonis
In horrore visionis)
For here the gaping mouth of hell
That yawns for them – and me as well.
Can we be saved before too late
And even now repel our fate?
Let's salvage this potential wrack
And strive to grasp what yet we lack!"


P ray bear in mind and keep some skill and wits –
There aren't such things as democratic *rits*.
*You* can't initiate them as you please;
They come, and only come, when 'Sir' decrees.
And now's the time to shed that precious 'T':
It smacks of Anglican gentility,
In fact the whole sound's rather middle-class
And, truth to tell, your vowels are getting *wahse*.
It takes but small adjustment as you glide
Between them with a mouth not over-wide…
If Basses sing with line, we'll all do that.
Sopranos, watch! That row of Gs goes flat;
Invest them with a forward purpose, please,
And Altos, try to summon brighter Es.
You Tenors need 'direction' there and 'presence';
You sounded like a bunch of rowdy peasants.
Mere decibels one always must berate,
*Piano*, though, does not mean scared and late.
The watchword for us all's 'Only connect!';
Transformed at once will be the whole effect.


O bserve how all these parts together slot,
Comprising one sublime melodic plot.
Savour the interaction as you sing,
The wondrous interweaving of the thing;
The voices feed off one another, strain,
Each against each, as in relentless pain,

And in the most despairing, crucial spots
The yearning anguish lies within the dots.
It seems as if all hopes and hearts would break,
The rhythm in itself transmits the ache.
So lock into this pulse, its urgent sob,
Its beating heart, its strong, compulsive throb.
(In bar-lines you should just suspend belief:
They're there exclusively to give you grief!)…
Like Russian dolls, or painter's sweeping brush,
These long, sequential notes are smooth and plush,
Joined at the hip, evolving without rush,
Like chocolate mousse, luxuriant and lush.
An even pressure travelling on
Like T'ai Chi in slow mo-ti-on,
Extraordinary drive and will
Yet glacier-like in seeming still.


Today I think we'll treat those Es as flat,
The B is natural there – remember that –
The Cs, though, should be sharp, so be alert:
On Friday we shall probably revert.
Though causing some dismay and others merriment,
It's good to play with them and to experiment…
How many problems come with tightened tongues,
As many as are caused by gasping lungs;
So breathe when 'blown' – don't strain till you go puce –
And keep those jaws and joints and tongues quite loose…
How I deplore a wishy-washy noise,
A solid wodge no listener enjoys,
Spaghetti blandness, lacking shape and spine,
Like brains made incoherent with much wine.
Each 'R' you must articulate and trill,
And all those lingering vowels you should fill.


"Thou'st heard all that, Lord: this I surely know.
Look graciously upon my aspiration
And in thy great munificence bestow
What I entreat: their musical salvation!"

© Jill Mitchell, 2006.

# CANFORD CHORALE (Jackman-style)

(To the tune of Ein Feste Burg)

Keep on the sunny side of the note:
Let major thirds be bright, not flat!
And *stop* that 'hoovering' in the throat.
Don't *do* that, please. Just don't *do* that!
First rule – Engage the brain,
(Unless you'd give me pain)
Put up your aerial next.
Preserve the flow of the text,
If it's syl-la-bic, it's inane!

Now some of you have no idea
How small's a falling semitone
Repeated notes – can you not hear?
May slither downwards like a moan.
Let's have a sense of goal.
Come on, we're on a roll!
Remember: Tick, Tick, Tick;
Do not get madly quick,
Just watch! For God's sake, have some soul!

15 August 2002

## LACOCK CODA

There's a dynamic which, it seems,
 Appeals to Anglo-Saxon phlegm:
Avoiding both uncouth extremes,
 It glories in the name of '*m*'.
  And thus it may be seen
  We love the Golden Mean,
   At all excess we chafe,
   Preferring to play safe:
Our style is bland, our tone serene …
 At counting we're not very bright –
  'A crotchet's one, a minim two!
  It's easier to get it right
 So what, my darlings, puzzles you? …'
 (Our entries are what whim dictates,
They swoop and waft like unmoored boats,
 Although we know he wants 'real notes',
  Not 'regional approximates')
 'That "goldfish" noise is quite absurd,
I don't need that! I cannot guess
  The sense of that in note or word;
  There is no music in such mess.
And I have seen, so help me God –
 Observing now such mental flab –
  More sparkle in the eyes of cod
  Slapped dead upon a Whitby slab!
Like rabbits caught in headlamps' glare,
 Seized up, bewildered and perplexed,
  Transfixed into a frozen stare,
Too late you see what's coming next.
  Let loins be girt, for pity's sake,
And stay more focused, and awake!'

Lacock Winter School, 2002-3

## AD MAJOREM TACTUS GLORIAM

Or, Making Merry with Andrew Lawrence-King

This fundamental principle hold fast –
This is the first of lessons and the last.
'Twas set by God in Sinai's mountain stone,
So it must throb through every vein and bone:
Without a sense of tactus
The rhythm's malefactus!
Feel this pulse and flail your arm:
This rocking pendulum shows calm
Assurance where the downbeat falls,
For ambiguity appals.
So please will you be extrovert and brave
And cultivate the Mexicana wave,
And focus on an inner sway and swing
So that you have real rhythm as you sing ...
Against confusion and distress
The tactus will insure us;
From mayhem, anarchy and mess
It will protect our chorus.
So through your corpus feel the click,
And with your fingers crisply flick.
My business (yeah?) is to instruct
But *you*, essentially, conduct.
Our safety rests upon the tactus,
Solid, rock-like and exactus.
And yet within is elasticity
And scope for plentiful plasticity.
Some rhythms are jaunty and pingy.
But others are expansive, slow and clingy:
For different accents there is room,
The instant, and the late-to-bloom.
Thus in Padilla's great motet
Your peroration will be poorer
Without a healthy drag on 'Et
Pro nobis Christum exora'.
On unstressed final syllables, make light
And early endings, for by contrast they
Highlight those places where the accents bite
And make the point in 'contrapuntal'way.
On quaver entries coming at the end
Of bars, determine boldly to suspend
The moment, then be swift – for that's the trick
Of that distinguished tenor, Layton Quick.

In triples, second beats take centre stage –
Chacona rhythms were the Spanish 'rage' –
And, bursting forth beyond the tactus tick,
The phrase would launch out on an offbeat kick.
But know precisely where the tactus sits.
To ward off shapeless and unscheduled rits,
I need you all to mark the basic beat,
Express this pulse with fingers or with feet,
With shrug, or gesture, sign, or yap or yelp –
Dear God! These people are in need of help.
Some of you still do nothing, so no great
Surprise you drift in vague, at odds, and late …
How otherwise can I express this thing?
Forget that cornett, Martin: come and *sing*!

**Coda:**

If there are bits you still don't know
And aren't quite sure how they should go,
You'd better *not* leave it to heaven:
The concert is tonight at seven!

Lacock, 31 July 2005

# FOR ERIK:

## GRATIAS TIBI AGO PROPTER MAGNAM GLORIAM TUAM!

How shocking when Erik van Nevel
Made clear to us his required *layvel*!
For from that first tea-time
We scarcely had free time—
He drove us along like the *dayvel*!

He constantly urged: "pay attention"
To every nuance he might mention:
In singular fashion,
With vigour and passion,
He moulded each ardent suspension.

Here was no *prima pratica* style—
*Seconda*, the thing! For a while
We forgot the charisma
Of mellow melisma;
Breathed energy, fireworks, and bile!

And all of us owned him a wonder
(As we stumbled from blunder to blunder)
For, with consummate art,
He sang every part
And showed us the splendour and thunder!

His text was explosive, frenetic!
How could he be so energetic?
Inspired, never tired,
For ever up-fired? ,
By contrast we looked quite pathetic!

But now the adventure is over,
And Erik, we hope, is in clover;
We're filled with elation
At such 'revelation'
And henceforth our *'ars'* will be *'nova'*!

Lacock: August 2001

# Ode to Erik  (or Erik in spate)

At first he said with baleful scowls:
"I need a good profile of vowels

And not these darkly English growls—
Sometimes so shapeless and so rude
As if they'd been already chewed
Or come from long way underground;
A nice and open 'Latin' sound
Is what I need from all around.

"Blow out a hundred candles on my sign
And then you will support your breathing fine,
Sustain your well-shaped phrases without lapse
For there is at this moment too much gaps.
Much singers take their breath without some care;
Remember Jessye Norman, full of air...
And I would beg of you, beseech,
Give me no Doppler effect upon those $C$s
But good in tune you place and focus each,
As you repeat them with a perfect ease...
Now, tip of tongue behind your underneath—
Oh, pardon me; I meant your underteeth.
And—even low in tessitur—there must be
A glowing, full-voiced, 'inward' quality
But, mind! We need good jumping here
That's careful, concentrated, clear,
For it is undisputed fact
That intervals must be exact;
These notes have very nice arrangements
Show expressivity on your changements.

"…Why is it, second choir, you still don't know
I told you stop a quarter hour ago?
Do not so lose yourself down in your book
That you forget you also have to look.
It would, I think, be better atmospheric
If you resolved to sometimes contact Erik!
I would be glad to have your condescension
I have a need for very much attention
(I am not ready yet to draw my pension!)
And on that painful, passionate suspension
Give me please, *please*, some real melodic tension…
I think we'd better stop, re-tune our *A*,
But not t'eorbo; that would take all day.
Now from the u'beat, u-*pp*-beat ninety-t'ree,
And be quite sure you keep your eye on me...
Almost at once you lose a bit
Of tempo; there is not a *rit*!
Ah, sing once more, please; that was wrong
*Laudate*'s not a cradlesong.
Invite you every people sing along
Be very-good-articulate, and strong.
As yet you give me not what I expect
For there must be much t'eatre in the text.
This is the angels' song which nothing quells;
You must explode like booming, pealing bells!
Here's no occasion for *cantabile*;
The heavenly band in glorious array
Exults with praise in the eternal day.
So with *attacca* let the words resound
And leave such feebleness back on the ground.

"If you take note of all these things I've said,
We'll send our audience tired, but glad, to bed!"

Lacock, July 2004

# SCHŰTZ-SCHULE

First and foremost, last and next,
Will you articulate the text,
For this is *Stile Nuovo* here,
Pronounce the message, crisp and clear!

More energy of speaking, please,
Pronunciation power!
And make immediately good music,
Don't take half an hour!

Be concentrated! On my sign:
*"Den tod verschlingt das leben mein"*—
You lose already time! Be strict!
*"Ich lasse dich nicht, lasse dich nicht."*

And Jesus' second name is *Christ*;
Sustain the phrase! *Ah, Heilge Geist!*
Es ist all hier ein jammertal,
Angst, not *und  trubsal uber all*!!

Now, second choir, take *up* your score
So that you see a something more
Of me also. I beg you try
More to remember: *Meet my eye!*

So, pay attent—no, take good note,
Be more enthusiast! *Oh, Gott!*
How often must I tell this choir:
Conviction, clarity, and fire!'

----------------o----------------

Thus Erik urged us on each day
And taught us how to sing and play,
And now our great dynamic leader
Can, with relief, go home—*in friede!*

Jill Mitchell. Lacock, 02/08/02.
(Second draft 17/09/09)

# A POLYMATH MUSICKMAN, ERIK

*ANTIPHON:*

If    on - ly your average cle-ric    could  sing        an in – ci -- pit  like  E ------- rik!

A polymath musickman, Erik,
Exacting, but never asperic,
Inspires each rehearsal—
From Machaut to Purcell—
Performance sublime, atmospheric!

With energy wholly generic,
Profound, and yet not esoteric,
His teaching is lit
By wisdom and wit,
Compelling, expansive, Homeric!

With smiling seraphic and spheric,
But impetus steely and ferric,
He drove us along
In celestial song,
His musical sights stratospheric!

You'd have to be an hysteric,
Or martyr to fever enteric,
(Malaise of some kind
In body or mind)
To resist this momentum mesmeric!

For rhyme's sake, he should hail from Berwick,
And relish the verse of Bob Herrick.
Alas, I can't claim
That as part of his fame;
But it is enough to be Erik!

*Repeat antiphon:* 'If only…'

Jill Mitchell

# WATCHING AND GELLING, WITH JEFFREY

Let's make a start and try this D –
No, listen to it properly,
It's clear that we don't all agree.
I'm sorry, but that note is duff;
Make sure it's really high enough . . .
All right. Now we are all on board,
Please hum a quiet D minor chord.
O dear, perhaps it's curt to carp,
D minor doesn't need F sharp.
O.K. Now let me hear a G –
I said a G, Jill, not a B . . .
And so, A major, choose your note –
C natural, though, won't get my vote.'

*Some tutors certainly have chid more*
*Than patient, roguish Jeffrey Skidmore!*


'Now you're up and almost running!
Still, it's not exactly stunning,
For some in private worlds are lost –
Which doubtless are exquisite –
But they ignore me at some cost:
Pray give MY world a visit!
If you aspire to function well,
Look and listen, watch and gel,
Lest you should fall into delusion,
Daydream, panic, rank confusion –
Now, how do you explain *that* glitch?
There was some talk of perfect pitch.'

*Conductors never teased or kid more*
*Than wicked, wily Jeffrey Skidmore!*

'Unless you focus and you think,
Be sure repeated notes will sink.
So concentrate: don't even blink
Commit yourselves and do not shrink,
And stretch those vowels to the brink . . .
It's early in the morning, though,
No wonder if your voices creak,
The brain is clear, the body slow,
The spirit's prompt, the flesh is weak,
Yet words must come alive and speak,
You might as well be singing Greek –
No sign yet of an early peak!'

*No maestro operates amid more*
*Merriment than Jeffrey Skidmore!*


'Be energetic in your diction,
Articulate with real conviction . . .
But, as I said, the day is young
And some of you are overhung.
At least it's clear you're not awake,
But cheers! Here comes the coffee break.
So, well refreshed, we're off again
But, tenors, spare me further pain:
Resolve to get a little closer,
Please at *più ferir non osa.*
Don't hurl yourselves with such a screech
As if that A were out of reach.
Sopranos, be more sensitive,
And much less piercing when you enter;
And basses, be less tentative
And strike that note clean in the centre.
Well, altos, what's amiss with you?
Let's go again from 32.
Don't hit the accents with great thumps,
The ear is battered by such bumps.
Just make a little mental space
And mould each phrase with ardent grace –
It's crucial that you shade away.'
In this vein we rehearsed each day.

*Few direttori ever did more*
*To make the music live than Skidmore!*

But we were struck with some dismay
When told about the Gallic way
The text must sound in Bouzignac.
We struggled to acquire the knack
Which, grasped at last, we could not cease,
So Frenchifying every piece!
Pronunciation, though, apart,
We made real progress in our art
And therewithal in right good heart.

*And so we make a fervent bid for*
*More future thrills with Jeffrey Skidmore!*

Zoagli, August 2004

A 'SLICE' OF SPICER:

Paul Spicer at  ZOAGLI, Liguria, September 2003


.. Now your crescendos really swell,
But still your 'dims' must 'tell' as well -
Quiet, impassioned.  Please don't yell!
And yet - bravo – it's going well.
Basses, it's that look of fear,
On your faces, ear to ear,
That makes me anxious to the core
And, yes, you've seen that bit before!
Be not wayward, do not dare,
Or else incur full-frontal glare! . . .
How pertinent we sing of hell
But, never mind, it's going well.
Now, make a virtue of that sixth
('My Bonny lies', a useful clue!)
And please ensure those thirds are bright
And give each interval its due.
Think 'tuning, tuning' all the time
Or sinking pitch becomes a crime,
And yet, well done for, truth to tell,
Despite the signs, it's going well.
Now, not so 'Nymphs and Shepherds', Sops,
We'll do without those breathless hops,
Just keep the tone sustained and free,
Your whole approach is somewhat twee.
Look, Basses, yet again you're late;
Give me an eye, not balding pate;
Be cleaner, please, upon that B
And when I 'rall', do come with me.
Just try to integrate your line!
But that was great: we're doing fine! . . .

# A READING FROM THE (POSITIVELY) LAST EPISTLE OF PAUL

## TO THE ZENNORITES

There's something empowering in triplets, I'd say,
They spring with such lilt and momentum.
When 4/4's in 6, don't go faint with dismay,
But make it quite clear that you meant 'em!
Crescendos demand not more volume but tone,
A richness and fullness, not loudness alone:
And all need to work on their cavernous yawn,
Producing a sound like a resonant horn.
But pure clarinet is the thing we need <u>there</u>,
Sopranos, that flowers and develops from air,
So *O, let the snowflakes* must grow from a dot,
Then blossom and swell…into all that you've got.

It's good to know that every Bass enjoys
That phrase, but it's a rather raucous noise
And manifestly tending still to sink –
Yet getting better all the time, I think…
Yes, Basses, that was absolutely right
As far as notes, but make your landings light,
Your timbre softer, your approach more 'kind';
That's fine – but you're a full beat now behind!
Just try to sing connected, growing lines
Not fragments, bits of jigsaw; use your minds,
For but a little thought will soon transform
A dull performance, lift the lifeless norm…
Let's renovate the Sops, now, for some voice
Is trailing like a tadpole – curious choice,
For blend and fine ensemble are your aim
And that's one reason, surely, why you came.
The Basses are improving by a thread –
A thread, though, that's detached, or almost so.
Please implement the things that I have said
And let the quality, not volume, grow.
Keep nurturing that tone throughout the Howells'
*Sing Lullaby*, while stretching all the vowels.
Now be alert and try not to annoy:
I warned I'd beat in <u>one</u> at *Wake and joy!*...
Be luminous on *lumen*; warm that *light*,
Sopranos, do not let your throats get tight;
At times there is an edge – don't push so hard
Or what would be a glowing sound is marred…
That bottom E in *Agnus*, Altos, vaunt it;
Don't be intimidated, or too shy,
For they that have it certainly should flaunt it –
Not up an octave, no; as writ! Let fly!

God! This rehearsal's left me like a wraith –
With pale and puny knuckles clenched on faith!

Jill Mitchell
Zennor, 31 Dec 2005

# 400 YEARS ON—IN SOLIHULL!

**Whatever might a more potent draw be**
**Than Monteverdi with Philip Thorby?**

"These Vespers—what a monumental piece!
Such headlong creativity outpoured,
Such stunning virtuosity displayed,
Is quite unsettling, almost frightening.
Amazing, see, the way the man combines
The *stile concertato* with the chant.
Chiaroscuro (Caravaggio!) sound
That utters shafts of dazzling light that arc
Across the sombre, dark solemnity.
How wittily he echoes the motifs
Of earlier genres, rhythmic shapes and forms
And sets off one convention with another.

Now, Singers, that's a Homer Simpson timbre;
Present me voices grounded, resonant.
Cast off, reject those louche Earl Greyish vowels,
Do not adulterate the Latin sound.
Eschew those twee and wetly English 't's,
Obtrusive consonants that block the flow.
Decline to be the framework; be
The main event! These long notes must have shape,
Direction, drive, then 'tripled' Alleluias burst
(Ensure this!) like Prosecco from the bottle.
Must I negotiate each single bar? —
The Muppets (disconcerting!) spring to mind...

Ah, Strings, 'the French Baroque' may not apply:
We're only on the cusp. What's more, I should
Explain to you a dotted crotchet makes
Three quavers in this psalm, so please oblige.
It's very ragged; more precision here,
Precision—mind! —and accent aren't the same.
Be more sophisticated, suave. Just think
Of me. Continuo: that passage lacked
A certain Je ne sais quoi... From the top!
But now it smacks of Walter Gabriel
And lurches with a quaint bucolic clump.
I need you to amaze me at this point:
A Major's luminosity should stun!"

**Although we often slipshod and raw be,**

**What pleasure it is (ywis) with Thorby!**


"Then *Sede* calls for full and sensuous tone,
Expansive and almost erotic here.
*Emittet*, Ladies, has a single 'm';
You well-nigh treble it, and sound as if
With utmost scorn you're slapping down the crude
Advances of a Tenor. Try again.
Now *Dominare* thunders through *in medio*
With uncompromising power, until
The ultimate in creamy sounds unfolds
In *genui*, where Father woos the Son.
But *Judicabit* thrills with menace, swords
Unsheathed and brandished. Armaggedon comes
At *Conquassabit* — yet the tranquil chant
Continues with unruffled, mystic calm.

He sometimes turns counter-intuitive,
But how electric in *Laetatus sum*
Wherein on *illuc*, such a humble word,
An adverb merely, Monteverdi sets
The various coupled voices to compete
In mimicry and wild parabola
Like two muezzins, vying each with each,
Across the rooftops. (*There* the tribes go up...)
Again, on *propter fratres*, comes the swirl
Of virtuosic, imitative notes—
A preposition only, but it thrills
And stresses kinship and community.
A minute later, in the selfsame phrase
Of *propter fratres*, crotchets 2 and 4
Must be metallic, pinging through and laid
Across the strong, sustained G Minor chord."

**On one-to-twenty, the 'score' must the score be
To sing these Vespers with Philip Thorby.**

"What brilliant picture next of wasted effort
For, nisi Dominus..., all is in vain.
Unfocused, flailing energy misfires
And *vanum est* and *frustra* urge the point...
Sopranos, why the implication here
That eating bread of sorrow is delight?
Your winsome charm is totally misplaced
For Nymphs and Shepherds are quite out of gear
When *manducatis* resonates with grief.
*Ecce hereditas* is too 'disturbed'
As if you had been shaken in a jar;
*Sagittae*, though, must loose those arrows off
With thrilling violence and deadly aim.

*Magnificat*—summation!—says it all...
*Misericordia* requires each Bass
To be a Chaliapin; but it sounds
Like bleary chucking-out time. Focus it!
Be purposeful, committed, powerful...
Why so depressed, Sopranos, to describe
The rich despatched with emptiness away?
(To me, I own, a quite appealing thought!)...
I have a problem, Tenors: in bar 2
Do you. sing *Gloria* or *gladioli*?
Which it is I simply can't decide,
While Cantus Firmus meditates aloft
With radiant insistence. *Sicut* is
Portentous and majestic and serene,
Its solemn import almost chills the spine,
And then, in bar 14, we melt in warmth
Of kindling sunshine, with the certainty
Of *nunc et semper et in saecula*.
Be gentle, sensitive. Do not apply
A red-hot poker to this music, please.

That final crotchet in the next-last bar
Will be as long or short as I decide
So take a risk (eyes out of scores this once!)
And shape that note to grow to where you sense
I'll place that crowning chord to seal **Amen**."

**Had we missed such riches, we'd clearly more poor be;**
**As 'tis, this work will for evermore be**
**Lit by the spirit of Philip Thorby!**

Jill Mitchell, April 2010

SNAPSHOT FROM UPHOLLAND, October 24, '98
(The long CORI SPEZZATI day ALMOST closes!)

A conversational-fragment overheard between a
soprano (doing a double-take) and the instrumentalist
who was doubling her line.

"Eh, what?  Reluctant though I be to carp,
That note you played – a 'natural' F sharp!!"

"Perhaps.  But you must grasp the problem that
This cornet's F sharp WILL be somewhat flat,
Especially when the trembling lip is tir'd,
And when the windy breath is near expir'd,
When cheeks are cramp'd, and drain'd one's vital pow'rs
By endless long and concentrated hours,
… Let's beg to differ, neither be the victor;
I'll plead to Bernard* he forgot the 'ficta'!"

                o-o-o-o-o-o-o-o-o-o-oo-o-o-o-


*Bernard Thomas, Founder/Director of the London Pro
Musica, Editor and Publisher of Renaissance music

# MUSICAL CHAIRS

This poem – a piece of uninhabited fantasy! – was written for the Lacock New Years's Eve party on the last evening of 2001. (The performance for which the whole course had been preparing – and was a typical 'Jackmanesque', eclectic mix of Guerrero, Ireland, Holst el al – was to take place the next evening in St Cyriac's church). It was inspired by a song called 'Place Settings' for which Jeremy Nicholas had written, words & music: he imagined a party in which innumerable, potentially awkward, individuals and couples have to be allocated seats with optimum tact.

In 'Musical Chairs' using a similar verse form and singing to Nicholas's notes, I imagined we were being joined by the various luminaries of the Early Music world, all converging on Andrew van der Beek's house and expecting to be fed. ('Lou' was our marvellous Lacock caterer at the time and 'Bertie', the supposed errand-boy, Andrew's younger son. 'The George' is the local pub conveniently situated at the end of the garden).

The fourth stanza adds to these a whole collection of accomplished Lacock conductors as if all were there simultaneously (not only Jeremy Jackman, the actual director that week).

High-spiritedly I brazenly 'lifted' the colourfully inventive 'frabjous' and 'frumious' from Lewis Carroll, knowing that Andrew would at once recognise and enjoy the theft.

# MUSICAL CHAIRS

We're having a New Year party;
    It's going to be a crush
'Cause everybody wants to come,
    So stand by for the rush!
Brace yourselves to greet them all,
    Remember who is who;
But how on earth to seat them all?
    We'll need the stairs – and loo!
    There are forty Tallis Scholars,
    The crème of Tudor crème,
With Peter Phillips standing by,
 All poised and set for 'SPEM!'
    The Gabrieli Consort
    Are here, The Hilliards, too,
And, look, His Majesty's Sagbutts are
    About to join the queue.

    The Early Music lobby
    Is gathering in force,
With Thorby, Lumsden, Hollingworth,

And Clifford B– of course!
There's Emma and there's Evelyn,
Whose brilliance none dispute,
And Anthony is hovering
And fingering his lute.
And here come Gothic Voices,
And there is Bowman (James);
Oh, what a wealth of choices,
And such distinguished names!
Then, braving the Atlantic,
Have come Anonymous Four;
Long-suffering Lou is frantic
And the kitchen's in a roar!

The goulash, couscous – all are done,
And vanished every quiche;
To cap it all, an argument's
Blown up round Paul McCreesh!
Is that John Eliot Gardiner
Still outside in the dark?
Amazing he could tear himself
Away from touring Bach!
Yes, do invite him to come in
And urge him through the door;
With luck he will distract them, and
Some harmony restore.
But, what's to do? The food's quite gone!
Dear God! How much they gorge!
So Bertie's sprinted through the grass
For pizza from the George!

There's a special 'Lacock' table,
And all the gang are there:
There's Edward come with Ghislaine,
Janjoost and Alistair;
There's Jeremy, and Nigel,
And Andrew Lawrence-King;
With Spicer and van Nevel,
It's going to be some 'sing'!
Now I spy David Lawrence, too,
And is that Matthew Rowe?
There, Kina, Duncan, Philippa,
And still the numbers grow!
Then Deborah R and Carlos,
And Jeffrey S. are here:
They've gone into a huddle now

To plan the coming year!

I think that's everybody …
But, no! What frabjous cheek!
How could I have forgotten
The frumious van der Beek?
How *could* I have forgotten
The frumious van der Beek?!

Lacock New Year's Eve Party 2001

# 'ONE-TO-A-PART' AT ROUJAN;  A CONSORTS WEEK

'Twas Anne and Fran's creative plan
That brought us all to Roujan;
With fear t'expose our timbre, we froze,
We nursed no more illoujan.
But, presque-vivre with joie-de-vivre,
We mark the grand concloujan;
So raise a cheer and come next year
For thrills in such profoujan.
(Though, being frail, we sometimes fail,
Are fearful of excloujan!).
But, come, let's broach another keg
For Tony, Robert, Fran and Greg.
YES, LET US CRACK A FINAL CAN
FOR ROBERT, TONY, GREG AND FRAN!

ORGANISERS;  Anne Roberts
& Francis Steele

TUTORS;        Francis Steele
Robert Hollingsworth
Anthony Rooley
Greg Skidmore

# THE WORD'S THE THING!

Sopranos relish runs and trills
In accents pure and fluty,
While Basses' boom the ether fills
With timbre bold and fruity;
The Altos strive for warmth of tone,
And richly graceful gliding;
The Tenor (Pavarotti-clone?)
Himself on head voice priding,
Aspires to lyric passion
In strangulated fashion.
And yet the WORD, the WORD's the thing
To which the NOTE plays second string!

Such is their joy in 'majored' thirds,
And each harmonic sea change
You scarcely can make out the words -
They're swooning on a key-change.
They are enamoured of their tunes,
They love melodic tensions;
You'd think their mouths were stuffed with prunes
When ling'ring on suspensions,
Their forte's not their diction,
The text becomes a fiction,
And yet the WORD, the WORD's the thing
To which the NOTE plays second string.

Let singers take for mantra;  IN
PRINCIPIO ERAT VERBUM!
All mumbling choirs commit a sin,
It's vital that we curb' em
For lazy singers to obscure
The message - what perverser?
They should illumine, make endure
The text, not vice versa,
Should focus mind, and heart, and tongue
To re-create each word that's sung,
Because the WORD indeed's the thing
To which the NOTE plays second string.

ENVOI
Be mindful, therefore, when you sing
The music, that the WORD is KING!

A response to a musical society's implication that some workshop participants were inadequate!

**ASPIRATION!**

'A man's reach should exceed his grasp or what's a heaven for?' – Browning

What comfort to know our Committee
Can sit, so it seems, smugly-pretty,
Upraising with sighs
Satirical eyes
Deploring that it's such a pity!
They've noticed that 'X" – and, yes, 'Y'! –
Have again had the gall to apply
To sing and to play
On a course, at a 'day',
"Debasing our standards!", they cry.
"Why will not these people aspire
To levels decidedly higher?
For – never an asset –
They're much better tacit
Than giving performance so dire.
Had they worked with assiduous graft
We would not have scornfully laughed;
But limited creatures
Should get themselves teachers
To help them develop their craft.
'Consorting' with such hoi polloi
Can do nothing less than annoy,
(For we are enlightened,
Our artistry heightened)
What is there in <u>that</u> to enjoy?
How favoured and blessed are we,
Endowed with such skills and esprit,
Whose talents are toned,
And carefully honed!
(You must in all conscience agree.)

With nurtured gifts and judgment we're imbued,
Secure within our own beatitude,
Which prompts us, like the Stratford Bard, to pen:
'How blest are we that are not simple men!'"

# CAROLS AND HYMNS

## Nos 25-50

## COME, O REDEEMER

(To the tune of *Salve Regina*)

Come, O Redeemer, splendour of the morning,
Come sun of justice, lead us out of bondage.
Come, holy wisdom, come down, Emmanuel,
Saviour.
Come, thou long expected, thy people await thee:
fill their hearts with glad thanksgiving.
Stretch forth thy hand, hope of all the nations;
dispel our darkness by thy word of love and truth;
be flesh among us.
Come Jesus, come Messiah,
born of blessed Mary,
and guide our joyful footsteps to salvation.
O, key of David, O flow'r of Jesse,
O shining day-star from on high,
bring the new dawning!

## BLEST THAT MAIDEN MARY

Blest that maiden Mary
Who, when she received
Heaven's shining minister,
In humble awe believed.

At his visitation
All her soul was stirred
As she heard on angel tongue
The Lord's amazing word.

Eyes and ears bewildered,
Mind and motion numb,
Yet in faith consenting that
Her destiny should come.

"See me here, His handmaid,
Let it be fulfilled;
May His purpose come to pass,
This wonder He has willed."

Blest indeed was Mary,
Grace was on her head.
God came down through her from heaven,
As Gabriel had said.

At this sacred season,
Praise the Mother-Maid
Who gave birth to God's own Son
And Him in manger laid.

Jill Mitchell

# ANGELUS AD VIRGINEM

Gabriel from heaven came,
An awesome message bearing;
Greeted Mary by her name,
Her destiny declaring:
"Hail, Mary, full of virgin grace,
To you all creatures shall give place;
Only believe,
You shall conceive
A Saviour,
The Lord of heaven and earth,
For God has looked with favour
Upon your peerless worth."

"How shall I conceive a child,
A maiden yet remaining?
How forget my solemn vow,
All truth and honour staining?"
"The Holy Spirit by his power
Shall bring to pass this timeless hour;
With joyful cheer,
Cast out all fear
And sadness,
For still virginity
Is yours, and yet this gladness,
By God's divinity."

Then the bright archangel heard
The voice of Mary saying:
"I accept the Father's word,
His messenger obeying.
God's secret purpose you have shown,
To me, unworthy, made it known.
The time is near,
His handmaid here
Behold me.
With faith I wait until
The things that you have told me
Are fashioned by his will."

Virgin Mother of the Lord,
Who, when you thus consented,
Peace to heaven and earth restored
And sin's effect prevented,
For us entreat your God and Son
That he forgive our evil done,
And grant us grace
To see his face
In glory,
As all the blessed do;
And may this Christmas story
For us be ever new.

Jill Mitchell

# GAUDETE
## (Words for Advent)

**Gaudete, Gaudete! Christmas is coming!**
**Bethlehem in starlight waits. Gaudete!**

Soon the Child so long foretold
In the prophets' pages
Will be here, to Mary born,
Longed for through the ages!          **Gaudete…**

Soon will hosts of angels sing,
Alleluias soaring,
Tidings of great joy will bring,
Then will kneel adoring.          **Gaudete…**

Raise your hearts and voices too,
Join the heavenly chorus,
Marvel at what Love can do,
God's compassion for us!          **Gaudete…**

For He sent us Christ, His Son,
Ultimate oblation!
Opening up to everyone
Prospect of salvation.          **Gaudete…**

To the Prince of Heaven and Earth
Honour, praise, and glory,
For He came in human birth—
Never-fading story!          **Gaudete…**

# WELCOME THE STRANGER   (Words: J Mitchell)

Welcome the stranger, there in the manger, Alleluia!
Baby and mother gaze on each other, Jesus, Maria;
Swaddling, not sable, clothes him in stable, Deo Gloria!
Oxen attend him, asses befriend him, Alleluia!

Nothing of splendour able to render Jesus, Maria;
In cowshed torpor born as a pauper, son to Maria.
Who would have thought it? But God has sought it! Deo Gloria!
This is his chalice, manger not palace, Alleluia!

Shepherds are hasting, no time for wasting, Alleluia!
Sheep may well need them, but angels lead them to Maria.
Bethlehem draws them, heav'n overawes them, Deo Gloria!
Speechless they honour Child and Madonna, Jesus, Maria!

We too adore him, kneeling before him, Alleluia!
Fact and not fable; there in the stable, Jesus, Maria!
Let us not falter, then, at his altar, Deo Gloria!
This incarnation brought us salvation, Alleluia!

**DREAM ON, CHILD**

(from the Natuatl carol 'Xicochi Conetzintle')


Dream on, Child,

Drowse gently,

Sleep safely,

Little Jesus.

At peace You slumber there

In heavenly hand.

At watch round Your crib

The great angel band,

Bright seraphim, stand.

Alleluia! Alleluia!

# PUER NATUS IN BETHLEHEM

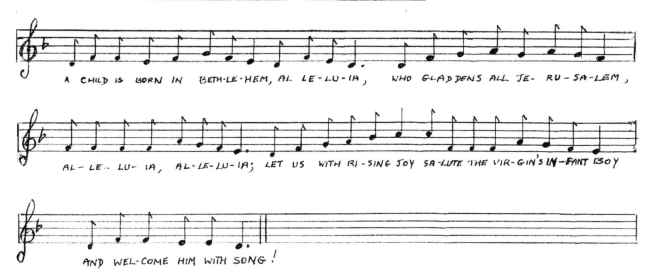

A child is born in Bethlehem, Alleluia,
Who gladdens all Jerusalem, Alleluia,
Alleluia;

> **Let us with rising joy**
> **Salute the Virgin's infant boy**
> **And welcome Him with song!**

The Son has clothed Himself with flesh,
Alleluia,
The creatures' manger is His creche, Alleluia,
Alleluia;        **Let us…**

In stable where the beasts attend, Alleluia,
Is He whose reign shall never end, Alleluia,
Alleluia;        **Let us…**

As Bridegroom from his robing-room,
Alleluia,
He came to us from Mary's womb, Alleluia,
Alleluia;        **Let us…**

The tidings brought by Gabriel, Alleluia,
Announced the Christ, Emmanuel, Alleluia,
Alleluia;        **Let us…**

When startled shepherds heard the word,
Alleluia,

They left their flocks to find their Lord,
Alleluia, Alleluia;        **Let us…**

And eastern Kings their camels spur, Alleluia,
To offer incense, gold, and myrrh, Alleluia,
Alleluia;          **Let us...**

They make their entrance, one by one,
Alleluia,
And reverence make to God's own Son,
Alleluia, Alleluia;          **Let us...**

Of Virgin-Mother was He born, Alleluia,
Who is the light of every dawn, Alleluia;
Alleluia,          **Let us...**

With Kings and shepherds, how we yearn,
Alleluia,
To see and marvel in our turn, Alleluia,
Alleluia;          **Let us...**

On His august Nativity, Alleluia,
The skies ring out festivity, Alleluia, Alleluia,
          **Let us...**

So we with adoration greet, Alleluia,
The Father, Son, and Paraclete, Alleluia,
Alleluia,

> **Let us with rising joy**
> **Salute the Virgin's infant boy**
> **And welcome Him with song!**

EXTRA VERSES FOR 'INFANT HOLY'

Starlight blazing! Wise men gazing
Tracked its journey night and day
To the stable, quite unable
To conceive a Prince there lay.
What were stranger than a manger,
Rustic, tender?  Here no splendour!
Scarce believing what they saw:
Infant-King on bed of straw!

Earth rejoices!  Angel voices
Add their rapture to the song,
Greet Messiah, the Desire
Of the nations, ages-long.
Scene so lowly, now most holy,
Life transforming, cold hearts warming,
Lord of earth and sea and sky,
In a manger, see Him Lie!

## TWO 'EPIPHANY' VERSES FOR 'THE WEXFORD CAROL'

Three Kings came marv'lling from afar,
They'd closely studied a strange new star;
It marked a great, momentous birth,
For God-made-Man had come to earth.
Above the stable at last it hung,
Where choirs of angels had lately sung;
Amazed, they found no lofty hall,
Nor palace splendour, but meanest stall.

Dismounting at the wooden door,
Wide-eyed, they entered, approached and saw
The youthful mother and her Son
And Joseph watching the little One.
Their costly offerings they unfold
Of myrrh, of frankincense, of gold,
Presented them with deep salaams
To Jesus, cradled in Mary's arms.

# FORTY DAYS AND FORTY NIGHTS

Forty days and forty nights
He was fasting in the wild:
Forty days and forty nights
Tempted, and yet undefiled.
Sunrays scorching all the day,
Shivering dews at night-time shed,
Satan lurking in His way,
Stones His pillow, earth His bed.

'If you are the Son of God,
Bid these stones transform to bread.'
"Man is nourished by God's Word,
Not by bread alone," Christ said.
Now the devil took Him high
To a towering temple wall;
'Dare to leap!  If you're divine,
Angel hands will break your fall!'

Undeterred, though twice he'd failed,
One more trick the devil played:
Took Him to a peak, from where
All earth's kingdoms lay displayed.
'If you serve me, all is yours,
Every realm and every throne.'
Jesus cried, "I'll hear no more!
Worship is for God alone."

Satan in disgust withdrew;
Angels came to Jesus' aid,
Ministered, and strengthened Him
As He fasted and He prayed.
So it was Our Lord prepared
For His awesome destiny;
Proof against what Satan had dared,
He went down to Galilee.

In this precious time of Lent,
May we keep all this is mind,
Deaf to sly temptation's tongue,
So we shall some wisdom find.
Lord and Saviour, stay Thou near,
Ever-watchful at our side,
That with Thee we may appear
At th'eternal Eastertide.

# A HYMN FOR HOLY WEEK

(To be sung to RVW's adaptation of Tallis' melody as in The New English Hymnal, number 373)

The Son of God laid down His life
To save our souls from loss.
This world, where sin and shame are rife,
He rescued by His cross.
But how can we that cost defray—
For nothing could suffice
To clear the debt and to repay
Him for His sacrifice.

They scourged Him, sent Him back and forth,
They used Him as a pawn,
They scorned Him as of little worth,
They mocked Him crowned with thorn.
When Pilate put it to the crowd
Christ did not have to die,
They chose Barabbas, shouting loud:
"This one we'll crucify! "

We know by faith, though did not see,
His anguish and His pain,
The taunting and the agony
Endured that we might gain
Forgiveness and eternal light:
When, gentle as a dove,
He meekly cast aside His might—
This was the God of love!

September 2013

## TO CALVARY OUR SAVIOUR CAME   (to the tune GONFALON ROYAL)

To Calvary our Saviour came
And on Himself he took the blame
For all our weakness, all our pride,
Our selfishness – for these He died.

And Judas, man of guilt, and fraud,
For silver pieces sold his Lord,
And in the garden, saying, 'This
Is He!' betrayed Him with a kiss.

They questioned Peter and he swore,
'I've never seen the Man before!'
He heard the cock, the hall grew dim,
And Jesus turned and looked on him.

Then Pilate to the crowd began,
'I find no evil in this Man',
And washed his hands to signify
He did not wish their 'King' to die.

But three long hours He anguished there
And offered up this urgent prayer.
'Forgive them, Father, everyone,
They do not know what they have done.'

For us He suffered, us He bled,
For us the Son of God was dead,
For we reject and we deny,
Abandon Him, and crucify.

Though men continue to betray,
Their Lord has washed their sins away
And if we seek His living grace,
We yet in heaven shall see His face.

# SAINT THOMAS

At evening that first Easter Day
The Risen Lord, in glowing calm,
Came to his friends, all hidd'n away
For fear the Jews meant further harm.

He showed to them His hands, His feet,
And pointed to His lancèd side;
Joyful at heart, they turned to greet
The living Christ who death defied.

He breathed upon them, gave them power
To free from sin the penitent,
Telling them all that from that hour
He sent them forth, as He was sent.

But Thomas was not with the rest;
Incredulous, he heard their tale.
"I'll not believe until I test
And see the mark of every nail."

And, eight days after, Jesus came
And as before He wished them peace,
Turning to Thomas, spoke his name,
And told him that all doubts must cease.

"My hands, my feet, my wounds are real.
Approach that you may well perceive;
Touch for yourself and see and feel
And be not faithless but believe."

With wonder, Thomas knelt to say:
"My Lord, my God, I know you now!"
Jesus admonished: "Blest be they
Who know by faith, nor reason how."

We cannot see our Risen Lord,
Like Thomas, gaze upon Him clear,
Yet we believe His Blood is poured,
His Body present with us, here.

Throughout our Christian history
This Sacrament has been adored;
Knowing by faith this Mystery,
We greet the Presence of the Lord.

Jill Mitchell.
For Saint Thomas's, Huddersfield.
Corpus Christi 1987

# THE GOOD SAMARITAN

Wherever true compassion is,
There Christ our Lord is at its heart;
But Priest and Levite scurried by –
They crossed the road, kept well apart.
The Good Samaritan took charge:
He saved the robbed and beaten Jew,
He bathed his wounds and tended him,
Did all that mortal man might do:
He took him to a friendly inn,
Arranged his care, then pledged to pay
Whatever else was owing still
When he returned along that way.
'Now do thou likewise', Jesus said,
'Resolve to imitate that man,
For every human being is
Your neighbour, kinsman, of your clan.'

The love of God enfolds each one,
Whatever background, class, or creed,
And we must love as He has loved,
Responding to each other's need,
Regarding neither rank nor race,
Including all in our embrace.

# BREAD NOT STONES

Bread not stones a father gives
When his children plead;
God more ever-ready is
To supply our need.
Oh, how much more
Is our Father in heaven
Ready to hear
All who call upon Him!

Flawed and graceless, yet we care
When our children cry:
Moved to pity their despair,
How could we pass by?
But how much more
Is our Father in heaven
Ready to hear
All who call upon Him.

"Ask!" He said. "I shall provide.
Search, and you will find.
Knock: the door will open wide."
Yes the Lord is kind,
And how much more
Is our Father in heaven
Ready to hear
All who call upon Him.

Healthy trees will proffer fruit,
Beautifying earth;
Men of Christ must follow suit,
Proving 'faith' in 'worth'.
They must respond
To their Father in heaven,
Ready to hear
When He calls upon them.

Twenty centuries-in-Christ
Should have conquered man,
Yet such time has not sufficed
To fulfil His plan;
So let us tune
To our Father in heaven,
Ready to hear
As He calls upon us.

Christians of the world, unite
In obedient love!
Purposeful, towards His light,
Let us firmly move.
With joy we turn
To our Father in Heaven,
Ready to hear:
Now He calls upon us!

Jill Mitchell

# KENOSIS

Fellow pilgrims now, no longer strangers,
Hesitation past and caution thawed,
Joyfulness and trust in Christ unite us,
Every mind and heart in true accord;
Of our common purpose let us weave
Another seamless garment for the Lord.

Creative man, in seeking truth and beauty,
Enlightens lesser men and gives them eyes,
Holds up the mirror to our fragile nature,
By his perception making them more wise,
Reflecting through his genius all things human,
Interpreting mankind in every guise.

We marvel and are humbled at this pageant
Of life presented with consummate skill;
But Jesus Christ was the incarnate Artist,
Depicting faithfully His Father's will:
Transcending self, He took the role of servant,
Enacting our Redemption on the Hill.

We pray to God that He may here inspire us
To take from Christ, His Son, Our Lord, our cue:
We too must empty us of self, becoming
The vessels of his will. May He imbue
Us with His grace and His humility
And, in His Love, design us all anew!


Jill Mitchell, 1990.

Based on Philippians 2:5-8.

(Written for the installation of a U.R.C. friend as
President of the Bolton Council of Churches.
The U.R.C. theme for the year was 'Christians Together'.)

English words to J.S. Bach's   BIST DU BEI MIR

O Lord, my God,
Stay close beside me
To bring me strength and comfort,
Greater faith and purpose,
When numbed by doubting or distress.

You came to earth
Solely to save us,
Redeeming us from evil,
Offering forgiveness
And the grace to put our trust in You.

In times of grief
You will sustain me,
And kindle me once more
With confidence and courage
And the will to lift my eyes again.

When sorrow comes,
You will refresh me
And cheer my downcast spirit,
Telling me of happiness
And showing me that life is good.

When sorrow comes,
You will refresh me.
Revive my flagging spirit,
Energise my weary soul,
And fill my heart anew with hope.

Enlighten my mind,
Help me acknowledge
I'm precious in your sight,
As is this earthly life,
And all our human years are truly blest.

OFFERTORY HYMN

Take, O Father, from our hands
Simple bread, and wine outpoured,
Offered now from loving hearts
To our true and living Lord.
In this place,
Grant us grace
That we may your plan fulfil;
All our sins and faults efface,
Strengthen us to do your will.

Jesus, sanctify and bless
These our gifts, and those who give,
Humble, penitent, we pray
That we may more fully live
In the light
Of your sight,
We who share your Godhead thus,
As you took our human plight –
Born of earthly flesh like us.

Let our prayer like incense be
As we lift the bread, the wine
In this Christian sacrifice
Where they will become divine;
May it rise
To the skies
To commend the offering
Which for our salvation cries
To our Lord, Redeemer, King!

# THOSE WE HAVE CHERISHED

Those we have cherished
Travel before us, and
Into the presence of
Jesus, the Saviour.
We who lament them,
Miss them and mourn them, take
Comfort that they are in
Everlasting rest.

God of gracious mercy,
Lord of deep compassion, we
Pray for the souls of the
Loved ones who have left us; their
Faith and hope commend them; let
Angels now attend them, and
Cherubim befriend them and
Lead them into light.

No more anguish,
Pain, or sorrow
there in realms of
Heavenly joy!
Grace and mercy,
Peace, and sweet forgiveness will
Welcome all those who put their
trust in the Lord.

Those we have cherished
Travel before us, and
Into the presence of
Jesus, the Saviour.
We who lament them,
Miss them and mourn them, take
Comfort that they are now
* United with the Blest,
And are in everlasting rest.

Jill Mitchell. May 30th 2018

*Extra line in last verse requiring repeat of last 2½ bars.*

For the beginning of the School Year

HYMN TO THE HOLY SPIRIT    (Tallis Canon)

Come, Holy Ghost, you who are one
With God the Father and the Son;
Come, Holy Spirit, and possess
Our souls with life and holiness.

Today we dedicate our year;
Send down, O God, your Spirit here
On each of us, that all we do
May show the strength we draw from you,

In will and action, mind and tongue,
With all our powers, your praise be sung;
In work and talk, in prayer and play,
Inspire and guide us through the day.

Diverse and many, Lord, are we
Yet make us all a harmony,
A unity though many parts,
Your spirit tuning up our hearts.

## HYMN IN HONOUR OF ST FRANCIS XAVIER

Written for St Mary's, Lowe House, St Helens

"Go out to farthest-distant shores
And spread my Gospel there.
For you shall teach all humankind
the mercy that they share."

Saint Francis took these words to heart,
he heard and he obeyed;
apostle to the Indian lands,
he ventured, undismayed.

With fearless faith and matchless zeal,
to highest and to least
he brought the light of Christian hope
in mission to the East.

He laboured long among the sick
and comforted their need;
he gathered crowds of old and young
and sowed the vital seed.

Committed to this great campaign,
alone and undeterred,
he harvested unnumbered souls
by his compelling word.

What dangers and distress he met,
what trials had to face,
but over all discouragements
he triumphed by God's grace.

Then, five years on, another goal,
a different scheme began,
new nations to evangelise;
from India to Japan!

Strange customs to be understood,
another language learned;
undauntedly he seized the task,
what high renown he earned!

And finally, off China's coast,
where he fresh conquests eyed,

ambitious to the end for Christ,
he sickened and he died.

His shining witness spurs us on
as we his life recall;
no more than forty-six brief years –
yet Francis gave his all.

For NOTRE DAME HIGH SCHOOL, St Helens, in commemoration
of the Canonisation of JULIE BILLIART,
the Foundress of the Sisters of Notre Dame.

## PRAISE GOD FOR SAINT JULIE

Praise God for Saint Julie, whose joyful vocation
It was to provide the deprived and the poor
With the blessing of Christian and sound education
Applying her vigorous love to fulfil
Whatever demands were made by God's will.

CHORUS   She read the signs of her time and answered its needs:
               Well aware what kills and what restores,
               She treated its ills and removed their cause
               With compassionate touch, and Saint Julie's way
               Applies as much to our world today.

She'd courage and energy, vision and hope,
'Oh we need souls of steel to be stable', she said,
'In the world that we live in, and then we can cope
With its crises, and deal with its dangers and dread.
Let's work for eternity, give of our best
In trust that our God will provide all the rest.'

'Remember', she said, 'we're the first and that those
Who come after will build on the stone laid by us.
What we need is a blending of drive and repose,
Of strength and of sweetness, of zeal without fuss.
Be ardent, but never escapist, in prayer:
We'll toil up to heaven, not be spirited there!'

How aptly designed for her own time and ours!
For we also live now in turbulent years
Of conflict, and tensions, and clashings of Powers,
And challenge of all long-established ideas:
By rallying banners of 'Freedom!' enticed,
We're scorners of faith and doubters of Christ.

For thirty years ill, and for many in pain
And unable to walk, - all the stronger her mind,
For God turned what looked like her loss into gain,
Made her spirit dynamic, her heart yet more kind.
In our lives, like Julie's, be thou adored
And magnified always, glorious Lord.

## O GLORIOSA VIRGINUM

O Glorious Virgin, peerless, blest,
Exalted over stars and sky;
You nourish with your kindly breast
The Child who lifted you so high.
      The grace that hapless Eve had spilled
      With your sweet Son is here restored;
      So heaven's aisles may now be filled
      And wretched man no more outlawed.
O portal of our great High-King,
Of Christ, the shining ante-room,
New-heartened, we rejoice and sing
Of ransom come through Mary's womb.
      All praise to Jesus, God the Son,
      Who deigned to be of Virgin born,
      With Father and with Spirit one
      Until the ages' final morn.

## INTEGRA, CASTA ET INVIOLATA

Most holy, chaste, and wholly without flaw,
By God appointed Heaven's gleaming door,
Benign and tender Mother of our Lord,
Accept the praise our grateful prayers accord;
And with your sweet persuasion, Mary, plead
That we too may be purified, and freed
In mind and body, by your lasting grace,
From all the faults that weaken or debase.
Most gracious Mary, Queen and Advocate,
Alone, you stand apart, inviolate.

# CANTICLE OF THE CREATURES
## (St Francis of Assisi)

Most high, omnipotent and holy Lord,
May You be ever honoured and adored
For You alone may praise and glory claim,
And worthy no man is to speak Your name.

May You be glorified in every one
Of these your creatures: firstly Brother Sun,
Who ushers in the day and brings Your light,
A radiant image of his Maker's might.

For Sister Moon and lustrous stars that blaze
In heaven, bright and beauteous, utter praise.
For Brother Wind, Signore, and for Air
In divers moods and seasons, harsh and fair,
Praise be, my Lord: for thus to all You give,
To every being, breath that he may live.

For Sister Water, vital, simple, sure—
We bless You, Lord, for gift so precious-pure.
For Brother Fire, who burns with sturdy light
To quell the shades and shadows of the night.

And for our Sister, Mother Earth, be praise,
For she sustains and orders all our days,
Providing us from richly-laden bowers
With fruits and herbs and many-coloured
flowers.

Praise be, my Lord, for those who, loving You,
Are able to forgive; and others who,
Enduring pain and sickness, trouble-bound,
Are yet at peace: by You they will be crowned.

Still be You praised, Signore, in the shape
Of Sister Death, whose coming none shall
'scape:
Alas for those who die in sinful case,
But blest be those she finds in state of grace
Pursuing still Your will without alarm—
A second death will scarcely do them harm.

So let us ever praise Him for our part
And serve Him gratefully with humble heart.

Jill Mitchell 7.9.09. post-Assisi.

## THE LAST PRAYER OF MARY, QUEEN OF SCOTS

O Domine Deus! Speravi in Te!
O care me Jesu, nunc libera me!
In dura catena, in misera poena, desidero Te!
Languendo, gemendo, et genuflectendo,
Adoro, imploro, ut liberes me!

Sweet Jesus, My God,
      My desire and my prayer,
Vouchsafe me, good Lord,
      To stay free from despair!
In harsh isolation,
      In painful privation,
        I strain towards you!
So, ailing and failing,
      I plead for your peace;
Adoring, imploring you:
      Bring me release!

# SUNDRIES AND OCCASIONALS

## Nos 51-72

## 'OUGH', what vagaries!

To start in rural mode, PLOUGH, BOUGH and SLOUGH
All rhyme with HOW, NOW, COW AND dog's BOW-WOW.

By contrast,  ROUGH and TOUGH, ENOUGH and CHOUGH
Accord with HUFF and PUFF, and CUFF and BLUFF.

The Irish word for lake, romantic LOUGH,
Evokes its Scottish version, LOCH, and BROCH,

But, O, U, G, H, as they are in THROUGH
Are vowel-identical with FEW and GLUE;

And OUGHT and BROUGHT and NOUGHT and SOUGHT and FOUGHT
Exactly echo WART and PORT and CAUGHT,

Then THOROUGH – more eccentric still! – and BOROUGH,
That have no rhyming twin apart from CURRAGH.

There's yet another sound in DOUGH and THOUGH,
That chimes with OH and GO and HOE and MOW,

Yet those four letters found in COUGH and TROUGH
Are bracketed in sound with DOFF and QUAFF!

And what I failed initially to PICK UP
There's yet another variant in 'HICCOUGH'!

Poor, hapless strangers can't make sense of this:
Pronunciation is so hit and miss,

And such reflections make it plain to see
How rich and strange is our orthography!

2006

# Anyone for Scrabble?

Come and join our game of Scrabble!
Test your brain amid the babble.
Can you think despite the din,
Plan your strategy to win?
Not so easy as it seems;
Bound, this game, to thwart your schemes....
Ah, a seven-lettered word!
Look, I've juggled to make 'spurred',
Bonus 50 to my score!
Never played seven tiles before.
Where, though, where to make it fit
The words that are already down?
Simply can't make use of it;
Frustrated, foiled, I fume and frown.
Infuriating there's no place
Where I can add it to the grid.
In no direction is there space.
I'll have to make a different bid.
And now 7 vowels is my lot –
Emphatically not my day –
Exchange some!   ....Look what NOW I've got –
Five 'I's, ye gods, a 'U', a 'J'!
Change tiles again, but keep the 'U'
In case I pick up blessed 'Q'....


Aaargh!   Anne's scored brilliant 48! –
And Marion, the ever-late,
Has just arrived.   What's now to do?
"We really had despaired of you.
But sit down.   Cup of tea and biscuit?
You've not altogether missed it.
We started long ago – a shame!
But soon there'll be another game."

But back to this one.  I must think
Where I can make a cunning link,
Scoring, perhaps, two ways at once;
Alas, I am a perfect dunce,
Can't see any clever move.
How on earth can I improve
My chances in this hopeless game?
I was quite upbeat when I came.


George is focussed and intent,
Pauline cheerful, confident;
Christine is relaxed and easy,
I alone am feeling queasy.
Theresa plays serenely on,
Passes tile-bag back to John;
Irene tells a tale and, after,
Everyone dissolves in laughter.

Oh, please let all the noise be stopped,
All my plans have belly-flopped.
All this chat's distracting me.
Where's that Scrabble Dictionary?
Does the word 'dolent' exist?
Yes, hurrah, it's in the list.
Good, I'll use it, Double Letter,
Double Word, too – even better.
Take more letters....here comes 'Q'
(Good thing that I kept that 'U')
'K', 'V', 'X' and 'Y'.  Curst luck!
Now I've really come unstuck,
For John has finished!  -As for me,
A minus-forty penalty!
AT LEAST THIS BEASTLY GAME IS DONE;
NOW MARION CAN JOIN THE FUN!

*There has always been a running joke amongst the members of Paul Olson's deservedly flourishing Poetry Group, a variation on the theme of "We're only here for the beer!".  Paul's wife, June, sends the most delicious apple cake to every meeting we have..............*

## FULL HOUSE

The poetry group is bursting at the seams!
Delighted at the crowd, our leader beams
Approval of the judgement and good taste
On which these growing numbers must be based.
The subjects and the themes this term impress
And whet the appetite; you'd never guess,
Though, that we're here, above all, for the sake
Of June's sublimely scrumptious apple cake!

We settle to the topic of the day:
It might be sonnets – 'darling buds of May' –
Or poetry of landscape, or of war,
The Georgians, the Romantics, days of yore,
Or verse that charts the modern urban scene –
Detached, prosaic, honest, brutal, mean.
If things get too intense, we start to ache
And yearn for that remaining piece of cake.

The tale has got around, you see, the word
Is noised abroad; the rank and file have heard
What sweetly toothsome pleasure they can glean
If they present themselves as madly keen
To dabble in the lore of poetry –
Its wit, its wisdom, its philosophy.
But this whole stance – admit it! – is a fake:
The reason for this groundswell is the cake!

When Hopkins' syntax seems a touch perverse,
Or modern cynicism even worse,
When poets seem to wallow over-much
Within their precious psyche's pains and such,
When contributions verge on the diffuse,
Or writer's diction seems un peu abstruse,
Or Eliot more than usually opaque, -
We salivate at the mere thought of cake!

The Ancients did this clear ideal proclaim:
A healthy mind within a healthy frame!
And, well we know, when intellect is tired
It is by June's confection new-inspired
For ravished taste-buds, as we always find,
To great effect do stimulate the mind:
The bright enthusings any of us make
Are prompted by the 'subtext' of the cake.

FOR NONE HAS BEEN DISCOVERED THAT CAN BAKE
TO SUCH EFFECT AS JUNE HER APPLE CAKE.

## Poetry Group Sonnet

This time last year I wrote a poem called FULL HOUSE, which sang the praises of the delicious apple cake that Paul Olson's wife June, makes for every meeting of the Poetry group: the burden of the song was that the cake, and not the verse, was the overwhelming attraction for the growing numbers. As this trend has continued throughout 2013, I thought it time to let loose a little counter-propaganda in the following sonnet!

### SONG OF DISCOURAGEMENT

About our Poetry Group, don't spread the word,
The crush of devotees is getting worse!
In wild enthusiasm they've concurred.
(Who'd have predicted such a vogue for verse?)
Such popularity's become a curse
And cries of "Where's a chair" all over heard.
"I'll bag this corner, dump my coat and purse.
Please guard my seat!" It really is absurd
The way they come, determined and perverse,
(What'er the weather, they are not deterred,
Though snow or deluge threaten to immerse!)
So we're commissioning a little bird
To rumour: 'IT'S NO LONGER UP TO MUCH.
AND WITH THAT FABLED CAKE, JUNE'S LOST HER TOUCH!!'

# NAME GAMES by Jill Mitchell

(Dedicated to Barbara, who loved the quirkiness of English place names.)

What images are conjured by our island's gazetteer,
That list of labels locative,
So colourful, evocative,
How maverick and queer!
How clownish or euphonious,
Absurd, sublime, harmonious,
The names of towns and villages unto my mind appear!
Let's take to G.K.'s 'rolling road'. (How tipsily we'll veer!)

To Samlesbury and Malmesbury, to Hooe and Smoo and Peover,
To Padbury and Cadbury, to Knill and Brill and Hever;
To Spridlington and Bridlington, to Wall and Saul and Seal,
To Feckenham and Beckenham, to Leek and Week and Deal;
To Shottery and Ottery, to Hook and Crook and Noke,
To Yarborough and Scarborough, to Liss and Diss and Stoke;
To Biddenham and Quidenham, to Lavendon and Lambourn,
To Ledbury and Sedbury, to Wavendon and Sambourne.
Godmersham, Rodmersham, Flimbury, Fring,
Amberley, Camberley, Limbury, Tring;
Scalloway and Galloway, Peckleton and Molesworth,
Tiddington and Piddington, Freckleton and Frolesworth,
Harpole, Yarpole, Palgrave, Tangley,
Hurley, Burley, Sulgrave, Langley;
Eagle, Meigle, Pamphill, Eccles,
Clapton, Slapton, Ampthill, Beccles.

To Broome and Frome, to Rede and Brede, to Laythes and Staithes and Stert,
To Nash and Flash, to Mere and Beer, to Toft and Croft and Churt.
To Rumbling Bridge, or Pluckley Thorne, Combe Florey, Cookham Rise,
Or Melbury Bubb, Pratts Bottom, Steeple Bumpstead, Aspley Guise.

But don't you love the 'yokel' names, like Stibb and Chalk and Cocking,
Crick and Crank and Kettlesing, Tumble, Clowne and Stocking,
Idle, Twatt, and Giggleswick, Stragglethorpe and Goring,
Seething, Wrangle, Brawl and Clink, Sliddery, Great Snoring,
Bonkle, Lank, and Evenjobb, Bunbury and Bobbing,
Dummer, Diggle, Dull and Drum, Fickleshole and Fobbing.

Though I will bet with confidence you'd give no jot nor tittle
For Ugley, Swine, or Maggots End, for Foulsham, Splatt Or Spittal;
Yet go to Chantry, Hassocks, Cross if sanctity you need,
Or Sacriston, or Rosarie, Allhallows, Steeple, Creed.
Addresses such as Pity Me, World's End, Bliss Gate, Farewell,
Good Easter, Christmas Common, have an aura, cast a spell.
Then there are names so lyrical they linger in the ear
Like Appledore and Lastingham, Tintagel, Haselmere,
Monksilver, Lydiard Millicent, Prickwillow, Ivinghoe,
Or Gamlingay, Lostwithiel and Chilton Cantelo,
And Wandlebury and Quethiock, and Margaretting Tye,
And Danby Wiske, Down Ampney, Saffron Walden, Barley, Rye.

On our affection and delight such places stake their claims,
How gauche, romantic, resonant this galaxy of names!

# '…THE MIND HAS MOUNTAINS…'

Exotic-sounding places fire
The routine action of the mind:
Imagination surges higher:
Tremors of romance inspire
Intimations unconfined.

Such sensuous sounds have always sung –
Mellifluous, alluring, strange –
Into my ear and on my tongue;
They have since I was very young,
Seducing me to dream and range.

With tapping, twitching feet and pulse astir,
I'm off to Vézelay and Vaucouleurs,

Cochin, Cuzco, Cochabamba,
Agra, Agadir and Amber,
Monterrey, Montélimar,
Zok, Zoagli, Zanzibar,
Tallahassee, Travancore,
Mevagissey, Mangalore,
Melk, Milwaukee, Manitoba,
Pondicherry, Pensacola,
Epidaurus, Luxor, Thebes,
Salamanca and Celebes,
Kalahari, Kathmandu,
Tetuan and Timbuktu.

Let me wave the classic magic wand
And conjure up the towers of Trebizond,
Philosophise upon its mystic strand,
Or take the golden road to Samarkand;
Stand silent on stout Cortez' peak in Darien
(Track down the several cities named for Marion!)
Or trace the smoke on dreaming Soufrière,
Or Flanders poppies at Armentières;
Be solemn with Empedocles on Etna
(Or – more bathetically – run off to Gretna!);
Go feel the breathing of Vesuvius,
Or gaze on fabled Troy or Ephesus;
Or, luckier than Belloc – who'd not gone –
Be awed by castellated Carcassone;
Or make that pilgrimage to Compostela
(Be warned: Galicia warrants an umbrella!)

Madurai and Marrakesh –
Even better in the flesh!
Ramillies, Rocamadour,
Joppa, Jasper and Jaipur;
Avallon and Angoulême,
So to Vespers at Solesmes!
Orléans and Orvieto,
Sparta, Spezia, Spoleto,
Sansepolcro and Siena,
Rare mosaic at Ravenna.
Cordoba, Cadiz, Casares,
Badajoz, Benin, Benares,
Coromandel, Rajasthan,
Shiraz, Kabul, Ispahan…

Fez and wistful Famagusta,
Ultima Thule and Finisterre
Glow with legendary lustre –
Venture further? Would you *dare*?

My father, not so privileged as I,
Saw only in his life an English sky,
But as in sleepy armchair he reclined,
Subsiding into well-earned evening ease,
He was transported to such spots as these
Upon the flying carpet of his mind.

Our hectic skies remove the need to guess:
The world's become our oyster – more or less!

© Jill Mitchell
27.11.05

## PENNINE WAYS

Full-blooded place-names,
Clotted with character,
Colour and custom!
Rugged philology
Layered with history,
Landscape and settlement,
Livelihood, culture;
Logjams of consonants,
Grit of the Millstone,
And clack of the clog!

Mytholmroyd, Thwackthwaite,
Lumbutts, Oswaldtwistle,
Heckmondwike, Beckwithshaw,
Scagglethorpe, Tintwistle,
Cleckheaton, Giggleswick,
Barnoldswick and Limbrick . . .

Clodhopping, clumping,
Ambling and stumbling,
Awkward and angular,
Limping and lumbering;
Often arhythmical,
Clumsily teetering,
Missing the beat
And dropping the stitch;
Wayward, wonky, walloping,
Loping, lurching, lolloping,
Gawky, gangling, gurning, gauche,
And, surely, anything but PÕSH!

Criddling Stubbs and Buttertubs,
Goosnargh, Grimethorpe, Gomersal,
Kimberworth and Cumberworth,
Copmanthorpe and Crumpsal.
Flushdyke, Fimber, Follifoot,
Thwing and Thwaite and Timble,
Sicklinghall and Heptonstall,
Crigglestone and Crimble.
Cockyard, Sparrowpit and Foxby,
Beal and Bugthorpe, Hive and Hook,
Ramsbottom and Wigglesworth,
Crayke and Clitheroe and Crooke.
Such tongue-twisters, you must agree,

Test anyone's sobriety!

There's Diggle, Dobcross, Duggleby,
Flash and Flagg and Flaxby,
Ughill, Unthank, Ouzlewell,
Humberton and Haxby;
Hebden Bridge and Halifax,
Hipswell, Horwich, Hessle,
Dishworth, Dallow, Dungworth, Drax,
Rawtenstall and Wressle;
Troy and Thimbleby and Tong,
Nab's Head, Nappa, Netherthong,
Gawthrop, Gamblesby and Gayle,
Bottoms, Birkin, Booze and Ayle! –
A rich syllabic tapestry,
Or overpowering pot-pourri!

Potent images abound
In this vibrant feast of sound:
An onomatopoeic throng
Of labels, comic, stark and strong
That bounce and stutter on the tongue.
(Impossible to be ignored,
A veritable treasure-hoard!)
How could they have remained unsung?

## STAYING WITH GRETA IN WANSTEAD

There's no room for divergent views
About a stay in Greenstone Mews:
Mine hostess could not be more kind,
With lively talk and thoughtful mind,
The warmest welcome, toothsome fare,
And plentiful ideas to share.
I ndeed, what tonic could be better
Than spending several days with Greta?

# MOVING HOUSE!

<u>RETROSPECTIVELY,</u>   of April 19th 1973. A friend's move to Huddersfield, recollected in comparative tranquillity later.


A wet coming we had of it,
Just about the worst day for a removal,
Such a damp removal.
The Pennines bleak, and the weather sharp,
The soul of moody April,
And the dog ignored, sore-bottomed, and desperate,
Squatting down in the boarded hall -
Young David, wide-eyed, pointing the enormity!
We almost regretted the whole venture,
Though silken Phyllis, heedless, brought us teabags.
Removal men meanwhile were humping and heaving,
And hinting that plurality of hands
Did not, ipso facto, lighten the load;
And Alan, recruited, threatening to run to 'The Shepherds'.*
A hard time we had of it.
Then at length we secured a temperate plateau,
Snug, past the pain-line, fragrant with oblivion,
For here was a tavern with vine-leaves over the lintel,
The trap in the kitchen revealing the treasure beneath,
It was, you may say, satisfactory!!

All this was long ago; but we REMEMBER!

* a nearby public house.

With apologies to T. S. Eliot

# THE LANGSTAFFS MOVE HOUSE

Now this is an auspicious date
For Jez, for Joseph and for Kate,
So may this 'res' prove really 'des'
For Joseph and for Kate and Jez
And may delight and pleasure grow
For Kate, for Jeremy and Joe.

So after all the toil and stress,
The seeming endlessness of mess,
The getting rid of so much junk,
The moments of unease and funk,
The times when courage almost fails
For ads on Ebay, car boot sales,

The packing up of crate and trunk
(The fortifying wine you've drunk!)
All's over now! In port at last,
And all the trauma safely past
And when you first engage the key
What jubilation for all three!

# REPLY TO AN INVITATION TO A FRIEND'S
## 70TH BIRTHDAY PARTY

No humdrum message: 'Thanks, we'll come!'
Could constitute an apt reply
On this august occasion;
So, sound a modest fife and drum,
For fitting 'tis that we should try
To answer with some 'blazon';
As invitations of such style
Demand that we should pause awhile,
And not respond in soulless prose
To words as eloquent as those!

The Lyons, Penningtons, and Swifts -
That's Richard, Kathleen, Joan and Bill
With Jim and Hilda - will be there
(Unless the snow whirls round in drifts,
Trans-Pennine traffic standing still
And glittering in the frosty air;
Or gales of eighty miles an hour -
As now I type! - should disempower)
And Dorothy, Joan G. as well
And Jill (who is implicit')
Declare that nothing short of Hell -
And possibly High Water,
Vouchsafing them no quarter -
Will suffer them to miss it.

We all look forward, with three cheers
To celebrate this feast of years
On March 9th, when we convene
With all of you at Woodsome Green!

## A Carillon for Christine

A truly memorable date
To mark and to commemorate,
A Ruby record we salute
Four whole decades have taken root!
Consistently, since eighty-one,
You have enhanced the liturgy
And played the 'King of Instruments'
With diligent fidelity.
All those years of parish music,
Aptly chosen, played with flair,
Christenings, weddings, requiems,
Always you were seated there.
Sunday Masses, Festal Days,
Echoing the cry of praise.
Each occasion brought to bear
Your sense of fitness, planning, care,
Building up the music's scheme
To reflect each special theme,
Choosing hymns that would accord
With what the readings had explored,
Keynotes of the Scripture heard
Rung again in tune and word.
Few there were who understood
What was required to make this good,
What this crucial role involved,
What the problems to be solved —
To search, inspect, reflect, reject,
Try out, correct, rehearse, perfect.
Most took for granted this was norm,
The way all organists perform,
But dedication so profound
Is somewhat thin upon the ground .
And so — one line for every year! —
Comes warm congratulation here.
For forty years we have received
Rich blessings from what you've achieved
By such sustained devotion driven,
So willingly and freely given.
With what distinction you have served!
*Bene merenti:* well deserved!


20 April 2021

## REMEMBERING DENISE

A lass of Sussex through and through
She breathes the landscape where she grew
And — showing me its rich delights,
From hidden gems to well-known sights —
She helped this Midlander explore
The charms of village, down and shore.
A seasoned walker, she would stride
(Some borrowed canine at her side!)
Down ancient paths, through wood and field,
From Houghton Green to Burwash Weald.
She loved the Great Outdoors, the feel
Of 'weather', be it rough or mild,
A panting comrade at her heel
Or, nose aquiver, running wild.
She thought all four-legged creatures friends,
So much of life on them depends,
And puppy, kitten, rabbit, calf,
She loved them all, they made her laugh;
It always was a soothing balm
To spend some time at Chilley Farm!

But onward marched both time and tide,
It's twenty years since I was there,
(Uncounted happy visits paid,
With memories that do not fade).
Denise was such a splendid guide,
Accompanying me everywhere:
To Cuckmere Haven, Winchelsea,
Bosham, Glynde and Pevensey,
Battle, Bodiam and Rye,
Arundel and Ardingly,
Michelham and Guestling Thorn,
Different plans at every dawn,
Spoiled for choice we were each day:
What road to take, to drive which way?

A loyal friend, her values sound,
With simple creed, and yet profound,
By all who knew her she is missed,
Abundant virtues crowd the list:
Her thoughtfulness and empathy,
Her reckless laugh, her gaiety;
Honest, thorough, conscientious,
No one could be less pretentious;

Kindness and delight in giving
Pleasure, all her zest for living!
Raise a glass and cheer her name,
Lives she touched are not the same!


December 2021

# CARPE DIEM

What are bodies for?
Bodies are where we live.
They make and unmake us,
They ache and they shake us,
They break and forsake us,
Display us, convey us,
Betray and dismay us
Time and time over.
They are to be glad in
But frequently sad in.
Where else can we live?

So strange a conjunction
It's odd, almost droll,
But thus do we function
As one awkward whole –
The body, the unction
Expressing the soul.

Think, if you dare to,
The ills flesh is heir to,
How fragile the case,
The dangers that face!
Precious, unique,
Much of life's wonder –
Attackable, weak,
So soon pulled asunder –
Fate's fickle thunder
Can strike at the peak.

The marvel of being,
Of thinking, of seeing
Survives, spite of all,
How priceless is life,
Though pitfalls are rife
And perils appal.
For wonder persists
And goodness exists
And hope, love an d faith
Are real and not wraith,
Through faltering and fall,
For long or short haul.

Take time by the scruff
And seize every minute,
There's never enough,
This second, begin it!
We're in this together
In all kinds of weather.
We'll not be reprieved,
Whatever achieved,
Must give and receive
Support, understanding,
Our lives thus expanding
As networks we weave,
While reaching to others
As sisters and brothers,
So do not delay:
Get hold of this day!

**Keeping the show on the road**

What is this life? A bleak affair,
If most of all one's time and care
Is spent applying balms and creams,
Inhalers, gels – ev'n in one's dreams.
With tablets, potions, possets, pills
For sundry interlocking ills.
Where is the time to "stand and stare" ?
The schedule has no time to spare..
"….at equal quarters through the day
Spread gel on tongue and use this spray,
But this pill must have two hours' grace
Before that capsule takes its place
Or I'm afraid you may expect
Some strange and unforeseen effect."
So watch the clock and concentrate –
Distractions will ensure you're late
With what the plot decrees comes next –
Don't answer door, or phone, or text
Or you will be at sea, in doubt
Just what it is that you're about.
Relentless tick-tock rules the day
And dominates the state of play –
But "play", in fact, is off the cards,
Frivolity's for fools – and bards.
*Divine Commedia* it's not;
It is the farce the Fates allot
To those whom modern medicine preserves
To test their patience, and their fragile nerves!

# UPON WESTMINSTER BRIDGE: MARCH 22$^{nd}$ 2017

Earth offers sights that sometimes tempt despair:
Villain or robot he would have to be
Who went unmoved by such atrocity.
This city now doth like a garment wear
The stricken shroud of mourning; people stare
At random bodies strewn, but others flee
While police and paramedics urgently
Address the carnage, under sirens' blare.
Little we thought a site of such renown
And cherished splendour could be so defaced.
This wanton rage defiles the ancient town
And fills our hearts with outrage and distaste.
But men of truth and honour must agree,
Despite it all, to strive for harmony.


*Jill Mitchell*

## A LINING OF SILVER: a little 'hymn' for Lynn and Tim!

Unloading half my shopping,
I lurched towards the door
And lost my balance in the porch
And ended on the floor!
One heavy supermarket bag,
Too much to lift at once,
Had totally unhinged my feet;
Why was I such a dunce?
I'd crashed into the redbrick wall,
Lay sprawled upon the tiles,
I'd wrenched my shoulder and left arm –
The shopping strewn in piles!
If you'd been passing on the road,
You might have heard a murmur:
'Whatever happened to the ground,
Why wasn't terra firmer?'
My plight seemed quite definitive –
Like frost, might well be perma;
Thin-skinned, indeed, my limbs and joints,
My ulcerated derma.
(For — yes!  — I'd greeted LOCKDOWN with
An ulcer on my skin,
For months it has refused all cure
And thrives upon my shin.)
But this was different: I was stuck,
My 'new norm' now was: flat!
I tried to wriggle round a bit,
Alas, no joy in that!
Then suddenly a stranger loomed,
He said his name was Tim,
He'd sped across, intent on help,
Thank heaven, I breathed, for him! ...
Despite all his endeavours, though,
No easy plan evolved,
He fetched a stool for me to clutch:
The problem stayed unsolved.
In fine, half in, half out the door,
I clung onto the stairs;
Both knees protested at the strain
On all their wears and tears
As I, still holding breath and hope,
Aspired to verticality;
One last huge effort won the day,
A semblance of normality ...

Throughout it all this unknown man
In circumstances fraught
Had raised my spirits, cheered me on,
And offered quiet support.
So now I've met my neighbours, Tim
And Lynn, but, how absurd,
For over twenty years so near
And no exchange of word!
How strange the way we live today,
So crowded yet encased,
Our better instincts stifled by
The cut–and–thrust, the haste.
But kindness and sustained concern
Have brought such dividends:
They've warmed the heart, lit up the week,
And 'strangers' now are friends!

5 September 2020

## PANDEMIC

So now at last the truth is crystal-clear,
That truth that Donne so ardently proclaimed,
That no man is an island in himself –
A solitary unit, snug, complete –
But everyone irrevocably bound
Together in the human family;
And all the quaint distinctions that we make
Of wealth or culture, colour, class or creed,
To which we cling to reassure ourselves,
Exposed for the illusions that they are.
The grim statistics cut us down to size:
Despite the progress made by human thought
–
Discoveries, inventions, power to heal,
The giant leaps that brilliant minds have made,
Amazing breakthroughs into realms of new
And endless-seeming possibility –
We know at last how fragile our control,
How vulnerable, finally, we are.
This enemy does not discriminate,
Cares not for prince nor pauper, no one is
Immune, none insulated from the threat
To democratic human frailty.

I think of some of those that I have known
And loved who died in safety, unaware
Of such a menace lurking in the wings:
They did not share this strangest of all times
When all our freedoms, norms and
expectations
Froze, and life was put on fearful hold.
We see more clearly than we ever saw
No action in the complex web of life
But has its implications for the rest;
Concentric circles ripple out from every
Move we make, at last affecting all.
The chain of being is so finely poised
That every link makes crucial sequencing
And wanton interference wrecks the plan.

Yet here, in this dark limbo, we observe
The selfless dedication to the sick
Of every nurse and doctor on those wards
In a vocation that requires reserves
Of courage and endurance past belief,
Devoted paramedics, care-home staff

Who risk themselves to tend the old and ill:
All these embody what is best in us,
The real humanity all lives must show.
And there are signs of new beginnings
On the civilian front. What irony –
When 'social distancing' keeps us apart –
That neighbourly behaviour has revived,
Imaginative acts of kindness shown
To those in isolation and in need,
While many thousands flock to volunteer,
To give their services which way they can,
To ease our passage through this painful time.

Our lives will never be the same again,
Indeed they must be 're-invented' as
Monsieur Macron has warned: huge
aftershocks
Will come, to private and to public life,
In mental stress and economic slump,
In lost employment, in a bewildered world.
We must emerge from self-obsessiveness,
Embrace our kinship with all humankind
(For all are members, every one of us
With every other, in this fellowship)
Call into question values we have held –
Pursuit of quick returns and slick solutions –
Look deeper to determine wiser goals,
And recognise our duty to the world.

Jill Mitchell

EASTER, 2020.

NOW JUST BEFORE THE LOCKDOWN
I bought a yellow coat;
My chance of ever wearing it
Is getting more remote.
I own that I already had
Three jackets of like hue
But each of them was different
And, honestly, that's true!
For one has velvet trimmings
And toggles that are black,
And one's a glossy floral print
While one of them's – a mack!
And, therefore, I could justify
This stubborn 'yellow' – phase,
And what could better complement
The daffodilly days?
But twinkling April is no more,
And blazing May has gone
And my new coat is languishing:
It's never been put on!

NOW JUST BEFORE THE LOCKDOWN,
A special birthday treat
Came in the shape of purple gloves
Which made my joy replete:
The softest leather, smooth and svelte,
Smart detail at the cuff,
What stylishness and elegance!
My 'cup' was full enough!
Yet they have never been to town
Nor seen the light of day.
My yellow coat and purple gloves
Are closeted away
While I am 'isolating' here
And under strictest 'shield'
And am condemned to twiddle thumbs
Till sentence is repealed.
Roll on the moment when it ends
And I can take the air
In yellow coat and purple gloves
And watch the neighbours stare!

CODA
But yet I sometimes wonder,

At a 'seasoned' eighty-five,
If on the first unpadlocked morn
When all the bolts have been withdrawn
I shall be still alive!

May 2020

## ST HELENS U3A: TEN YEARS ON!

Who will not cheer this milestone date,
Ten fruitful years to celebrate,
A decade since that daring day
St Helens launched its U3A?
Eight hundred plus, our numbers show,
And over fifty groups in tow.
With choices wide, how it has flourished,
Needs supplied and talents nourished!
Arts and crafts, a range of sports,
Some keen debates, exchange of thoughts,
Fancies and reactions aired,
So much fun and laughter shared,
Diverse aspirations fed,
Body, spirit, heart and head.

How decide to spend your leisure,
Play the Chimes, or Sing for Pleasure,
Knit and Natter, Colour, Chatter,
Weaving beads, or sowing seeds,
Playing Chess, or ukulele,
Stage a concert, or a ceilidh,
Write, read, study, act or play,
Hard to choose from such array,
Try a language, know the thrills,
Get more 'techno', hone those skills,
See great buildings, watch a show —
All the time the options grow.
Satisfaction without measure,
Rich experiences to treasure.

So at this time of Covid gloom
(While thousands strive to master 'Zoom'!)
We look beyond the stress and strain
To when we reconvene again
To flex our limbs, our soul, our brain;
As we contribute, we shall gain
For all will profit as they give,
Together, as we LEARN, LAUGH, LIVE! *

(* 'Learn, Laugh, Live' is the logo of the U3A)

September 2020

## THE LURE OF THE LIMERICK (Where is the 'remote'?)

I've developed a regrettable habit recently, when I eventually get to bed, of thinking about limericks. The writing of one is an excellent discipline because it concentrates the mind on getting the scansion right (a dying art!) and sharpening the rhymes (another one!). It is, however, extremely irritating when the perverse brain resists the 'off' switch and refuses the desired oblivion. I wrote the following three during the past week and tweaked them a little in the cold light of the following morning.

A 'clever clogs' student from Lyme

Responded to questions in rhyme.

Her tutors protested;

One sharply suggested

A better recourse would be mime!

A dizzy young hack from Penzance

Penned stories of such wild romance

The tales that she set down

Made real life a let-down

She thought she'd cross Channel to France!

A woman who lived by the Humber

Bought dresses, hats, shoes without number.

At length she saw sense

And resolved to dispense

With half her encumbering lumber.

I've decided to stop this addictive and pernicious practice,

For sleep, increasingly, is a consummation devoutly to be wished.

So, as;

> These persons are Lyme, Penzance, Humber
>
> Are quite unconducive to slumber,
>
> I'll ponder instead
>
> When laying down head
>
> On poppy fields, sheep - or cucumber.

I am afraid I didn't manage to quench the 'limerick' impulse. We have some delicious place names in this country and there came a moment when I couldn't resist STOKE POGES. Then there's PORLOCK, full of literary resonance suggesting challenging, offbeat rhymes. When the poet Coleridge was living in Nether Stowey, Somerset, he was unexpectedly visited one morning by 'a person from Porlock'. The night before he had had, he claims, a vivid dream in which he had experienced the whole of a colourful, exotic poem KUBLA KHAN. On waking he was frantic to write it down before he forgot it all. He had completed just thirty lines when this visitor, an insurance agent I think, arrived. This interruption totally wiped the slate of his memory and we are left with a beautiful and sensuous fragment. The idea of 'persons from Porlock' signalling the death of the Muse has been referred to by innumerable writers since, among them the great Vikram Seth who uses 'porlock' as a verb to mean to kill another's inspiration.

I have had, and continue to have considerable trouble with my new door lock so I use this detail with feeling!

An unfriendly pair from Stoke Poges

Were dubbed by the locals 'the Bogies'

But, though they were charmless,

The couple were harmless

And nothing but pompous old fogeys.


A cunning old person from Porlock,

Reputed a bit of a warlock,

I begged to attend to,

And please put an end to,

My moody, malfunctioning door lock!


A young altar-server from Kent

Foreswore sweets and football for Lent

But, mad about all sports

And liquorice allsorts,

He soon was obliged to repent!


And a final one for music buffs.

An Alto who sang in a Schola -

Her name? Oh, I think it was Lola –

Loved rhythmical ruses

Like threes – into- twosies,

Delighting in each hemiola!

### A PAEON FOR JUBILEE

Once upon a simple time
We held our moral frame secure,
Our values strong, our leaders fine,
A guarantee that would endure
And, looking at less favoured climes,
Would scorn, 'Here, you'd not find such crimes!'

But this is the time of tumbling icons,
This is the day of fractured dreams,
So many assumptions proved illusions -
What IS so rarely is what SEEMS -
Our expectations culled to size,
The scales have fallen from our eyes.

Good men, thank heaven, in every sphere
Remain – committed, true, sincere -
Who focus on the role they fill
With steady, dedicated will:
But others have betrayed our trust
And trampled principles to dust.

But this is the time for jubilation
Over Commonwealth and Nation
For 'constant as the northern star'
One woman stands, an exemplar:
She pledged herself with heart and nerve
To wear the Crown to shield and serve.

Though made in innocence and youth,
That promise has become the truth:
That, whether life were long or short,
Whatever future that it brought,
Whichever way events should turn,
Her people would be prime concern.

These seventy years have borne this out,
Her probity not once in doubt,
Through national and personal pain
Her grace and leadership remain,
With courage and humility
For each eventuality.

So, after this unprecedented while,
'God bless and keep her!' Let the prayer be fervent,
A tribute to a queen who opts to style
Herself now, still, 'Elizabeth, your servant.'

February 2022

c

Printed in Great Britain
by Amazon

84404849R00066